a garden project workbook

the

kitchen garden

a garden project workbook

the
kitchen garden

Richard Bird

photography by **Jonathan Buckley**

STEWART, TABORI & CHANG
NEW YORK

Text © 2000 Richard Bird
Photography © 2000 Jonathan Buckley

Design and photographs copyright
© 2000 Ryland Peters & Small

Published in 2000 by
Stewart, Tabori & Chang
A division of U.S. Media Holdings, Inc.
115 West 18th Street
New York, NY 10011

Distributed in Canada by
General Publishing Company Ltd
30 Lesmill Road
Don Mills, Ontario, Canada M3B 2T6

ISBN: 1-55670-960-9

A CIP catalogue record for this book is available from the Library of Congress.

Produced in China by Sung Fung Offset Binding Co., Ltd.

Composed in New Baskerville.
10 9 8 7 6 5 4 3 2 1
First Printing, 2000

Designed and edited by **cobalt id**

Illustration **Richard Bonson**

Project co-ordination **Paul Tilby**
Production **Meryl Silbert, Patricia Harrington**

Art Director **Gabriella Le Grazie**
Publishing Director **Anne Ryland**

contents

Kitchen gardening combines the production of fresh vegetables and fruit for the kitchen with the aesthetics of the ornamental garden; it is tasty and pretty, making it one of the most satisfying forms of gardening.

There is nothing like the taste of fresh fruit and vegetables. The fact that you pick or harvest your own produce just minutes before it appears on the table means that your food has a flavor and freshness that you will never get from a grocer. Until you have grown your own, you have missed a culinary experience that will top all others.

Vegetables are decorative plants in their own right, and many of the artifacts used in vegetable gardening, such rhubarb forcers, add to their visual impact. Some vegetable gardens are created specifically for their attractive qualities, but even those laid out along more traditional lines will give a great deal of pleasure. There is no need for a huge space when planning a vegetable garden: big areas undoubtedly have the advantage of large-scale production, but enough can be harvested from the smallest gardens to make the effort worthwhile.

This book sets out a series of projects that contain both inspirational and practical ideas for gardens of all sizes—from a roof garden to a large plot. Even a patio without any visible soil can be turned into a productive area. The plants given in the following plans and lists are suggestions only; please use your own favorites to create more personal gardens.

Richard Bird

right Cages that provide protection from birds should not be used just for fruit; many vegetables also need guarding. Here an attractive mixture of vegetables, fruit, and vulnerable flowers is grown in a home-made cage.

below Even very common vegetables have varieties of ornamental value. Lettuces, for example, are available in a range of reds and red-browns, and with differently shaped leaves, including feathered and frilly forms.

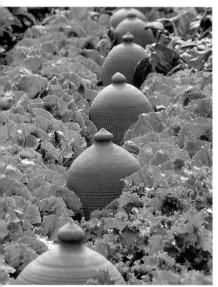

above Large flower pots, old-fashioned cloches, rhubarb forcers, and even scarecrows can be used to break up expanses of vegetation in the garden. Here a row of terra-cotta pots nestles among endive.

vegetable, fruit, and herb plots

A vegetable garden, or potager, is more than just a means of growing vegetables. It can be very decorative in itself, and is often the ideal solution in a garden where space is at a premium. A plot can be anything from a simple rectangle with rows of vegetables to a more complex potager, in which every plant is carefully positioned to create a satisfying and balanced picture. The garden can be broken down into various areas, each with its own purpose or decorative quality. Herbs can be grown in a knot garden, for example, or strawberries can be grown within rectangles of low box hedging. The possibilities are endless.

above Mixing flowering plants with vegetables adds another dimension to the potager. Here lavender bushes line a beet bed.

left Fruit trees add vertical interest to a kitchen garden as well as forming part of the permanent structure. They also, of course, provide fruit.

below This potager features a strong symmetrical design, prominent ornaments, and vegetables and herbs that are allowed to flower.

potager

A well-maintained vegetable garden is decorative in its own right; however, it is possible to go one step further and produce a kitchen garden that is not only productive but also designed to look attractive. There are many ways to do this, but basically it is a question of combining the colors, shapes, and textures of plants in a well-considered layout. Paths, beds, and ornamental structures can all play valuable roles. Such a garden may be a single bed or a combination of several.

materials & equipment

terra-cotta pots
gravel
edging bricks

spade
fork
rake
trowel
pegs and string
bottle and light-colored sand
measuring stick
watering can
garden roller

vegetable seed and plants in variety
plenty of well-rotted organic material

5 mature vegetable plot
Try to keep the potager looking its best throughout the summer. Harvesting plants leaves gaps that can upset the design, so keep a few young plants growing in pots and trays to serve as replacements. Quick-germinating, fast-growing crops, such as radishes, which can be sown *in situ*, can also be used as fillers.

plant list

1 sweet peas
2 lavender
3 alpine strawberries
4 mizuma greens
5 tarragon
6 hyssop
7 French sorrel (in pots)
8 lettuce in variety
9 rhubarb
10 Florence fennel (finochio)
11 standard rose
12 cardoon
13 apple mint
14 sage
15 rosemary
16 curly-leaved parsley
17 squashes
18 flat-leaved parsley
19 ruby chard
20 atriplex
21 bush tomatoes
22 climbing rose
23 chives
24 leeks

filling gaps in the design
Terra-cotta pots can be planted up and placed either as a permanent part of the display or to temporarily fill a gap. Keep several pots in reserve to use whenever there is a blank space or to replace a pot that has finished.

1 planning

Draw up a plan of your desired potager.
In the first instance it should include only
the bare bones and permanent features
of the vegetable garden, including paths,
edging, and any hedges and trees.

2 marking out the plot

Thoroughly prepare the plot by removing all weeds and moving existing
plants that are in the wrong place. Transfer your drawn plans to the ground
using pegs and string. Curved lines may be laid out using lengths of flexible
hose. Double-check all measurements—they must be right the first time.

3 laying the edging and path

It is not essential to fix the paths permanently in concrete; indeed, you may
wish to enlarge or redesign the potager after a few years. To keep your
options open, simply firm down the soil in the path areas with a garden
roller and roll in several layers of gravel. Alternatively, lay paving slabs
on a bed of sand. If using gravel, put the brick edging in place before
laying the path.

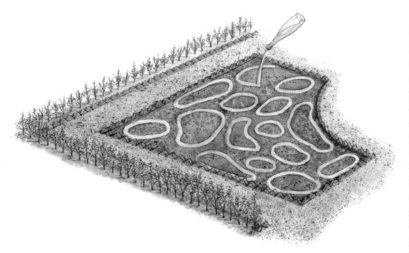

4 planting

Dig the bed areas, adding
as much organic material
as possible. Draw out the
planting plan on each
bed using a bottle
of sand as an oversized
pencil. Sow the seed
or set out the plants
according to your needs.
Planting a box hedge
around the potager will
give it a distinct boundary.
Set out the young box
plants at 6 in (15 cm)
intervals (see page 23).

traditional vegetable bed

The traditional vegetable plot is usually arranged in rows. It is set out for practical rather than aesthetic reasons but, carefully planned, it can be visually attractive as well as productive. The sheer variety of leaf forms and colors, as well as variation in height and breadth, creates a decorative pattern that is difficult to better. Gaps between the rows allow for easy access to the vegetables, both for cultivation and for harvesting.

materials & equipment

spade
fork
rake
hoe
pegs and string

vegetable seed and plants in variety
well-rotted organic material

1 preparing the ground
Prepare the soil thoroughly in the autumn, digging in plenty of well-rotted manure or compost. In spring, rake the soil surface to give a fine tilth. Use a garden line or string and pegs to mark out rows for planting, ensuring that there will be sufficient space between the rows when the plants are mature.

2 sowing
Most seeds can be sown directly outdoors; follow the guidelines on the packet. Some can be broadcast onto raked soil, then lightly covered over; others should be sown into a narrow drill (see page 19). Plants that are grown close together, such as peas, should be sown two abreast in a wider drill, about 10 in (25 cm) across, made using a hoe.

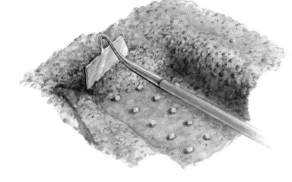

3 protecting the seeds
After sowing in a drill, cover with netting to protect the seeds from birds. Covering the soil with an organic or plastic mulch helps retain water and chokes out weeds, greatly reducing the time needed for cultivation. Organic mulch, such as grass cuttings, should be applied between the rows once the seedlings have become large enough not to be smothered.

4 watering
All vegetable seeds and seedlings should be kept well watered; many, including the brassicas and lettuces, need intensive watering for a good crop. Using a seep hose laid between the rows cuts down on labor; the hose can be moved easily across the whole vegetable patch.

5 extending the growing season
Depending on your zone, the season for vegetables such as spinach, peas, and brassicas can be extended well into autumn and early spring by growing them under cloches. For example, spring cabbage planted under cover in October will be ready in February. Lightweight, plastic cloches are available, but it is worth seeking out glass ones that will enhance the character of your garden.

6 care and maintenance
A low box hedge around the bed improves the garden's appearance but has no other practical value. A taller hedge or fence is needed if shelter from winds is the goal. The vegetable bed should be kept well watered and regularly weeded. Crops grown under a cloche require extra watering, and any plants started under cover should be hardened off before exposure to the elements, otherwise their growth may be stunted.

plant list

1 cabbage
2 brussels sprouts
3 tomatoes
4 leeks
5 onions
6 peas (on supports)
7 potatoes
8 kohlrabi
9 turnips
10 spring cabbage
11 celeriac
12 snap beans
13 shallots
14 flat-leaved parsley
15 lettuce
16 parsnips
17 beets

salad bed

All vegetables are best appreciated when fresh, and salad plants in particular are crispest and most full of flavor immediately after picking. Growing your own lets you harvest as much or as little as you want, and allows you to combine, in a single salad, the flavors of a wide variety of lettuces. If bought from the store or market, this culinary effect would be prohibitively expensive; added to this is the great satisfaction of growing your own vegetables.

materials & equipment

spade
fork
rake
hoe
garden line or pegs and string
trowel

seed of salad vegetables in variety
well-rotted organic material

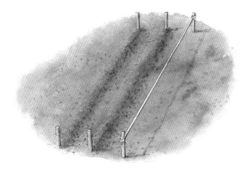

1 marking out the plot

Prepare the soil by digging thoroughly and working in plenty of organic material. Using a garden line, mark out the rows allowing for the size of the full-grown plant plus 12 in (30 cm) between each row for easy access. If you do not have a ready-made garden line, pegs and string can be used in the same way.

2 planting

Using the edge of a hoe, make a shallow channel, or drill, along the lines marked out. Scatter seed evenly along the drill, cover with soil, and firm down gently before watering. In very wet conditions, line the drill with dry sand before sowing; in dry conditions water the drill before sowing and lightly press the seeds down into the soil.

3 thinning and watering

Even when sown sparingly, most salad crops will need thinning out. When the seedlings are big enough to handle, pull out surplus plants, leaving single plants at the required intervals (equivalent to the width of a mature plant). Any check in growth will affect size and taste—so keep the plants well-watered in dry weather to ensure that they grow continuously. The best method is to water each row individually with a watering can, making certain that the soil is thoroughly soaked.

4 salad throughout the year

Salad crops are needed year-round, but if lettuces, for example, are sown at once then they will crop together and be over in two weeks or so. Rather than sowing full rows, is better to sow part of a row every two weeks. Many loose-leaf lettuce varieties resprout to give a second or even third crop when cut at the base. Such cut-and-come-again varieties are an excellent way of making use of limited space.

5 sowing radishes

Harvesting salad crops inevitably leaves ugly gaps in the rows. To make the best use of space, these can be filled by sowing radish seed; radishes are quick to mature and are ready for the kitchen just three to four weeks after sowing.

planting celery

Dig plenty of manure into the soil—celery demands high levels of nitrogen. Raise young celery plants from seed in the greenhouse. In the spring, set these small plants out in a narrow trench.

6 pest control

Perhaps the most destructive salad crop pests are slugs, and you must reduce their numbers or there will be little left for you to eat. An effective way to kill them is to set a beer trap—a jar, partly filled with beer, set into the soil. Alternatively, simply remove the slugs from the plants at night, when they are most active.

blanching celery

When the celery reaches a height of about 12 in (30 cm), wrap corrugated cardboard around the stems, leaving the leaves free. Fill the trench with earth, drawing it up around the cardboard sleeve.

7 maintenance and harvesting

Hoe along the rows and around each plant to remove weeds. Leaf vegetables cannot be stored; cooked pureed tomatoes can be frozen; celery can be left in the ground until needed.

plant list

1 scallions	**6** radish
2 beets	**7** cucumber
3 radicchio	**8** celery
4 romaine lettuce	**9** tomatoes (staked not bush)
5 loose-leaf lettuce	

strawberry bed

Although strawberries are widely available from stores all year round, nothing tastes quite like those eaten straight from the plant. Strawberry plants are relatively inexpensive, easy to grow, and look attractive whether in a bed or grown together in a container. With careful selection of varieties, they can be harvested from late spring right through to the autumn. The fruit is suitable for eating as it is, preparing for meals or drinks, or turning into preserves.

materials & equipment

posts, flower pots, and netting
straw for mulching

spade
fork
trowel
rake
garden line or pegs and string
measuring stick
hedge clippers
watering can

7 boxwood (*Buxus sempervirens* 'Suffruticosa') per 3 ft (1 m) of hedging
5 strawberry plants per 6 ft (2 m) of strawberry row
2–3 buckets of organic matter per square yard (1 m)

1 preparing the bed
Mark out a plot using pegs and string, checking that the corners are right angles. An area of about 15 x 10 ft (4.5 x 3 m) will provide a generous crop.

2 planting the border
Strawberry beds look attractive if they are surrounded by low hedges or raised boards. Plant young box, preferably a dwarf variety such as *Buxus sempervirens* 'Suffruticosa', in the spring at 6 in (15 cm) intervals around the bed. Pinch out the tips so that the plants bush out, which may take several years. Keep the box clipped back to the height and width required.

3 planting the beds
Prepare the ground thoroughly by removing all weeds and digging in plenty of well-rotted organic material. In late summer, buy plants that are guaranteed free from disease. Plant these at 16 in (40 cm) intervals in rows that are 2 ft (60 cm) apart. Water thoroughly; keep watered until they are established.

4 mulching
In the late spring, just as the fruit is beginning to swell, mulch underneath the plants with straw, tucking it up under their leaves and stems. This helps keep the fruit off the ground. Alternatively, black polyethylene can be placed under each plant.

raised bed
A board surround to the strawberry bed not only looks good but is easier to prepare than a box hedge border. The bed can be built up by filling in with plenty of well-rotted compost and good quality loam, creating a fertile growing medium for the strawberries. The board edges also help to prevent straw in the bed from being blown or scattered.

pole fence
An alternative to a board is to use hazel or chestnut poles. These should be 1 in (2.5 cm) in diameter and split in half lengthways, then nailed to uprights that have been driven into the ground, or woven between them. Low woven hurdles can also be bought as ready-made panels.

5 protecting your crop
Ripening fruits are a target for birds in late spring. To protect your strawberries, place short posts in the ground and drape netting over upturned flower pots—these allow the net to be moved without damaging the mesh. Weight the netting at the base.

6 mature beds
Pick the strawberries by pinching through the stalk to avoid bruising the fruit. Strawberry plants will begin to deteriorate after three years on the same soil, so it's best to position your bed so that other crops can be rotated in.

taste of Asia

Traditionally, vegetable gardeners are a very conservative species, adopting new plants rather slowly. For example, both potatoes and tomatoes took several centuries before they were widely grown in Europe. But in recent times gardeners have become more adventurous, matching the exciting developments in the kitchen and restaurant by growing more and more exotic and asian vegetables.

materials & equipment

bricks
¾-in stone
concrete
2 x 4 in (5 x 10 cm) wood for frame
1 x 1 in (2.5 x 2.5 cm) wood for runners
2 x 2 in (5 x 5 cm) wood for frames of lights
galvanized screws
glass cut to size
glazing points and putty
wood preservative or paint

spade
bricklayer's trowel and line
level
saw and router
hammer
screwdriver
ruler and pencil
fork and rake
pegs and string

seed and plants in variety

1 growing under a cold frame

Many asian vegetables can be grown successfully under cover in a temperate climate. A cold frame built on a brick base provides a warm and permanent environment. To build the brick base, first use pegs and string to mark out a rectangular trench 6 ft 10 in x 5 ft (210 x 150 cm) on its outer side, and 10 in (25 cm) wide. Dig down to a depth of 16 in (40 cm) and remove the soil.

2 building the walls

Ram down 5 in (13 cm) of ¾-in stone in the base of the trench; pour and level 4 in (10 cm) of concrete on top. Lay two courses of bricks below ground level.

3 completing the brick enclosure

Build the rear wall so that the top is 24 in (60 cm) above ground level. The front wall should be 17 in (43 cm) above ground level. The side walls should slope between the two. The "steps" in the top of the side walls can be filled with cement to create a smooth slope.

4 assembling the top frame

The top frame should be made from 2 x 4 in (5 x 10 cm) timber, cut to fit exactly the dimensions of the brick enclosure. Join the vertical and horizontal members by sawing out a section from each, half as deep as the timber itself, and as wide as the opposite member.

5 joining the members

Use two screws to join the shorter vertical timbers to the longer horizontals. Arrange the screws on the diagonal—if they are in line, they are likely to split the wood

6 the frame

Treat the frame with preservative, or paint it with primer, undercoat, and topcoat. The frame can then be screwed onto the top of the brick enclosure

7 attaching battens to the frame

Nail wooden battens 1 x 1 in (2.5 x 2.5 cm) to the shorter cross members. These will prevent the lights (the glazed panels of the cold frame) from sliding sideways when fitted later.

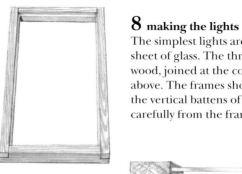

8 making the lights

The simplest lights are rectangular wooden frames that hold a single sheet of glass. The three frames are made from 2 x 2 in (5 x 5 cm) wood, joined at the corners with halved joints, made as described above. The frames should be just wide enough to fit snugly between the vertical battens of the frame—make your measurements carefully from the frame itself.

9 glazing

Using a router, cut narrow ledges, or rebates, into the edges of the frame to hold the glass. Fit a sheet of horticultural-grade glass that has been cut to the correct size by a glazier. Secure using glazing points and putty.

10 planting

Dig the soil at the base of the enclosure, mixing in well-rotted organic material. If this soil is not particularly deep, good garden soil or potting compost can be added on top. Sow seed lengthways across the frame in shallow drills. Stagger the sowings so that crops mature at different times. Thin as necessary.

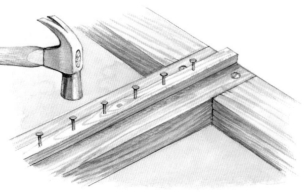

11 maintenance

Leave the lights open as much as possible, but put them on to protect the crops during cold weather. The plants will need regular watering, especially around the edges where rain may not reach.

plant list

1 garland chrysanthemum 'Large Leaf'
2 mustard greens 'Southern Giant'
3 mustard greens 'Red Giant'
4 bok choi 'Choki'
5 Japanese celery
6 texsel greens
7 garland chrysanthemum 'Small Leaf'
8 mustard greens 'Green in the Snow'
9 choy sum 'Purple Flowering'

raised vegetable bed

Using raised beds in a vegetable garden is a very old tradition that has recently found favor again. The advantage over conventional beds is that there is an extra depth of good soil, allowing the plants to put their roots down in search of moisture and nutrition. The beds are designed in such a way that they can easily be reached from all sides so that there is no need to walk on and compact the soil—a big advantage.

materials & equipment

bricks
concrete
3/4-in stone
good loam

spade
shovel
level
garden line or pegs and string
tamper
builder's trowel
wheelbarrow
fork
rake
trowel
hoe

seed and plants in variety
well-rotted organic material

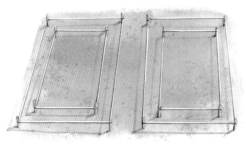

1 planning the beds
Think carefully about the construction of the raised brick beds. They should be just wide enough so that the center can be reached from either side, and there should be adequate space to move between them. They should be in a sunny but sheltered position.

2 laying the foundations
Dig two trenches forming rectangles 6 in (15 cm) longer and wider than the proposed beds. They should be 10 in (25cm) wide and 16 in (40 cm) deep. Ram down 5 in (13 cm) of 3/4-in stone in the base and then pour and level 4 in (10 cm) of concrete on top of this.

3 building the walls
The walls of the beds are brick; they are easy to construct and look attractive, but they could equally be made of concrete blocks, which are quicker to lay. Build up the walls so that there are two courses below ground and four above—about 12 in (30cm) higher than the surrounding soil.

allowing for drainage
Once the soil in the bed has been dug, water should drain away easily. But to ensure that no water gets trapped within the walls, a vertical joint should be left uncemented every 18 in (45 cm) when laying the course of bricks at ground level.

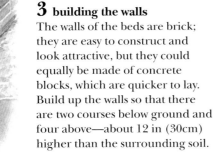

4 ground preparation
When the cement has hardened, prepare the bed. Kill or remove all traces of perennial weeds. Dig the soil to at least one spade depth but preferably double-dig it to two, being careful not to bring any subsoil into the top layer. Add plenty of organic material.

5 filling the beds
Once the existing soil in the beds has been cleaned and dug, add a mixture of good quality topsoil (loam) and well-rotted organic material. Fill the beds right up. Do this in autumn and allow to winter over. Top up with more soil and compost in spring.

6 path between the beds
The area between the beds needs to be kept clear for easy access. To prevent it becoming a mass of weeds or a muddy track, it can be covered with paving stones.

7 planting
Vegetables can be planted in blocks or rows. If you cannot reach directly into the center of the beds, lay a plank between the rows to walk upon. Left in position, planks will also help keep the weeds down and retain moisture.

plant list

1 seed beds	7 turnips	13 tomatoes
2 leeks	8 beets	14 zucchini
3 fava beans	9 parsnips	15 bush beans
4 parsley	10 rutabaga	16 celery
5 lettuce	11 alpine strawberry	17 cabbages
6 carrots	12 lettuce	

right There is no excuse for tired and limp lettuce when you grow your own in containers on the patio just outside the kitchen door. Cut-and-come-again varieties are best; those with colored or frilly leaves not only look delightful on the plate but make for highly ornamental potted plants.

container-grown fruit and vegetables

Growing food for the table is a practical proposition even in the smallest of gardens. Most vegetables, fruits, and herbs can be raised in containers as long as they hold sufficient growing medium and are watered at least once a day. The best container crops are those that produce edible leaves or fruit continuously and so do not create gaps in the display when harvested. Plants with colored fruit—such as tomatoes—or those with ornamental flowers—such as climbing beans and zucchini—are worth considering.

above Strawberries are an excellent fruit for growing in containers. Even a small pot will yield a daily handful of berries. The key to success is regular watering and covering with netting to prevent bird damage.

right Citrus trees in pots make good specimen plants and can be used, like these orange trees, on either side of a doorway, gateway, or steps, or on the patio. They are tender and need to be moved inside for the winter. Outside they do best in a warm, sheltered position.

above Cooks recognize the convenience of keeping fresh herbs close to hand, making them ideal patio potted plants. Many, such as these thymes, are happy in small, shallow pots as long as they are regularly watered.

above Tomatoes can be grown very successfully in pots, but need support. In deeper containers, canes can be pushed into the compost; otherwise a framework outside the pot with string supports works well.

left With few exceptions, herbs are not strong enough personalities to grow as single specimens. They look much more effective when grouped together to allow their colors and textures to mix.

rooftop kitchen garden

As space becomes increasingly precious, every square inch has to be used to best advantage. Living in a top-floor apartment in the center of town seems to preclude any chance of growing vegetables, but by making use of a flat roof, you can create a productive kitchen garden. Restricted access to a roof space means it is easier to build planting containers *in situ* rather than moving ready-made structures into place.

materials & equipment

For each bed:
8 lengths of 2 x 2 in (5 x 5 cm) timber, 2 ft 6 in (75 cm) long (legs)
12 planks of 1 x 6 in (2.5 x 15 cm), 2 ft 6 in (75 cm) long (legs)
12 planks of 1 x 6 in (2.5 x 15 cm), 3 ft (90 cm) long (sides of beds)
4 planks of 1 x 6 in (2.5 x 15 cm), 2 ft (60 cm) long (ends of beds)
6 sections of 2 ft x 3 ft 2 in (60 x 95 cm) CDX plywood (floors of beds)
12 lengths of 2 x 3 in (5 x 7.5 cm) wood, 3 ft (90 cm) long (side bearers)
12 lengths of 2 x 3 in (5 x 7.5 cm) wood, 2 ft (60 cm) long (cross-bearers)
16 lengths of 1 x 1 in (2.5 x 2.5 cm) wood, 12 in (30 cm) long (inner leg slots)
galvanized screws
wooden trellising

two foot square
saw
drill
screwdriver
hammer
level
hand fork and trowel

young plants and seed in variety
garden soil
well-rotted organic material

1 assessing the space

Before starting, consult a structural engineer to confirm that the roof can withstand the weight of the garden and will not be damaged by walking and working upon it. On paper, carefully plan out the position of the beds, containers, and any furniture needed for the garden, leaving plenty of room to move around. The design of the beds is modular, so the wood can be cut to length on the ground and taken piece by piece to the roof and assembled. Nevertheless, building a rooftop garden is a major undertaking.

2 choosing your vegetables

The rooftop garden shown here centers on two raised beds, each 9 ft 6 in (285 cm) long and 2 ft (60 cm) wide. The beds are 30 in (75 cm) high, allowing for easy access; beneath each bed is a shelf that can be used for holding pots and seed trays. This is just one possible planting scheme.

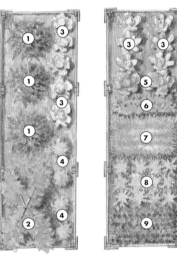

plant list

1 tomato	6 radish
2 climbing bean	7 scallions
3 lettuce	8 carrots
4 basil	9 beets
5 cabbage	

3 making the frame legs

Make the frame of each bed from wood that has been treated with preservative. Each of the eight legs consists of a 2 ft 6 in (75 cm) piece of 2 x 2 in (5 x 5 cm) wood. Screw a 1 x 6 in (2.5 x 15 cm) plank to the outside face of each of the four central legs using galvanized screws.

the corner legs

For the four legs at the corners of the bed, screw two 1 x 6 in (2.5 x 15 cm) planks to the outside faces of the leg. The planks provide surfaces to which the side-bearers of the bed can be fixed.

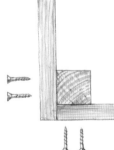

4 attaching the side-bearers

Screw lengths of treated 2 x 3 in (5 x 7.5 cm) timber to the protruding lips of the planks to create the side bearers, which will support the weight of the soil in the bed and the shelf below. They should be attached so that the upper tier of side-bearers is 18 in (45 cm) above ground level, and the lower tier is 6 in (15 cm) above ground.

5 adding the cross-bearers

To complete the frame, cross-bearers should be fitted. These are 2 ft (60 cm) lengths of treated timber, 2 x 3 in (5 x 7.5 cm) in cross section. Screw these into the side bearers of the lower tier at intervals of about 18 in (45 cm).

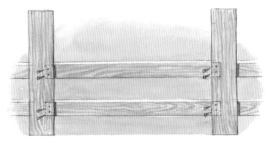

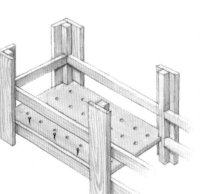

6 making the floor of the bed and the shelf

The lower shelf and base of the raised bed are cut from 1 in (2.5 cm) thick waterproof CDX plywood. Drill holes at regular intervals to allow water to escape. Starting with the lower shelf, screw the plywood to the side bearers and cross bearers. Next, fix cross-bearers to the upper tier and screw on plywood to make the floor of the bed.

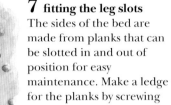

7 fitting the leg slots

The sides of the bed are made from planks that can be slotted in and out of position for easy maintenance. Make a ledge for the planks by screwing lengths of 1 x 1 in (2.5 x 2.5 cm) wood to the leg uprights. This creates a slot wide enough to take a 1 in (2.5 cm) wide plank.

8 slotting in the sides

The 1 x 6 in (2.5 x 15 cm) side and end planks are then cut to length and slotted into position. Two planks, one resting on the other, make a bed 12 in (30 cm) deep.

9 filling the bed

Cover holes in the plywood base of the bed with old pieces of pot so that water can run through, but soil cannot. Cover the base of the bed with small stones. Fill the bed to three-quarters maximum depth with good quality loam, or topsoil mixed with garden compost or manure. For deeper-rooted vegetables, fill the bed completely.

10 maintenance

Look after the plants as you would in a conventional bed. Add fresh organic material periodically. This may necessitate the removal of some existing compost, although this will shrink as it breaks down. Every three years, empty the beds and treat the timber with a non-toxic preservative.

basket of tomatoes

In a small garden, every square inch can be exploited to produce vegetables. Vertical space can be filled using hanging baskets and window boxes; and with careful choice of plants, the baskets can be attractive as well as productive. Here tomatoes have been mixed with flowering and foliage plants, but they can equally be grown alongside other vegetables if space allows. Several baskets in a group, hung at different heights, make an impressive display.

materials & equipment

basket
liner
galvanized eye and hook
compost
slow-release fertilizer or liquid feed

basket waterer
trowel
pruning shears

1 tomato 'Tumbler'
2 petunia (*Petunia* 'Purple')
2 variegated Swedish ivy (*Plectranthus coleoides* 'Variegatus')

1 preparing the basket

Hanging baskets are available in a range of materials and designs. Wire baskets are inexpensive and light, but wrought iron, terra-cotta, wicker, or wooden baskets may be preferred for aesthetic reasons. Before a basket can be filled and planted, it must be lined.

2 lining

Fit the lining, which may be of fiber, molded paper, moss, or polyethylene; the last is ugly if not completely covered by plants. The lining should be porous, so drainage is not a problem. It is easier to work on the basket if it is supported on a bucket, particularly if a heavier basket is used.

3 filling the basket

Hanging vegetable baskets look their best when completely covered with plants, so it helps to plant the sides as well as the top. Use a craft knife to cut holes or slits in the liner before pouring in the compost. Make the holes no bigger than necessary to push the plant through.

4 planting the sides

Partly fill the basket with compost to just below the level of the slits in the lining. Wrap the roots of the petunia plants in damp tissue to prevent damage, then push the young plants through the holes in the lining, spreading their roots. Fill the basket with compost. Petunias make a decorative display, but productive plants such as lettuces can be substituted.

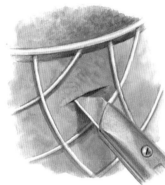

5 planting the tomato

Plant the tomato in the center of the basket, so that it will hang down on all sides. One of the best tomatoes to use is a variety called 'Tumbler', which has been specially developed for planting in hanging baskets.

6 hanging

Baskets with tomatoes should be hung in a warm, sunny position. If there is an existing beam, then a stout eye screwed into the woodwork will be enough support. Be certain that the beam is strong and in good repair. The basket can be hung at any height that seems appropriate. Lower is easier for care and maintenance, but baskets usually look best when above eye-level.

7 watering and feeding

Hanging a basket above head height makes watering difficult. One solution is to use a pump-action water dispenser with a long, bent lance. Unless it is raining, baskets should be watered at least once a day; twice on hot days. They also need regular feeding. A slow-release fertilizer can be incorporated in the compost, or liquid feed can be added to the water. Harvest fruit as it ripens and remove any that is damaged or over-ripe.

8 grouping baskets

Vegetable baskets look especially attractive in groups of three or more. Hang them at different heights for the best effect. For variety, hang one basket below another.

salad basket

As an alternative to tomatoes, plant the basket with cut-and-come-again lettuces. There are varieties available with red foliage and with crinkly and oak-leaf-shaped leaves. A surprising number can be included in the basket if planted around the sides as well as on top. The result will be a ball of colorful lettuce.

patio container garden

Even the smallest paved patio can be transformed into a kitchen garden. Anywhere that provides a small area for standing containers is enough to produce a few crops. Quantities may be a bit restricted but the quality of fresh, home-grown produce will be abundantly apparent. As well as producing vegetables, fruit, and herbs, a patio kitchen garden will be an attractive feature if well designed. Virtually any fruit or vegetable can be grown, although the less rampant varieties are preferred.

materials & equipment

variety of terra-cotta pots
potting compost
broken pots or stones
2 ft x 2 in (60 x 5 cm) plastic drainpipe

pick ax
spade
fork
trowel
pruning shears
drill

plants in variety

1 preparing for planting

The average patio provides many opportunities for planting crops for the table. Conventional terra-cotta pots are attractive, versatile, and free-draining; larger containers can be made from half-barrels; and many vegetables thrive in grow-bags. Spreading plants are best planted directly into the ground: use a pick ax to lift a few of the paving slabs.

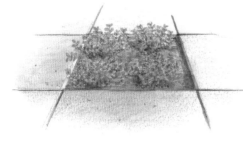

2 ground plants

Remove any rubble and sand from beneath the lifted slabs. Break up the soil below this and then fill the remaining space with fresh soil or compost. Plant spreading herbs such as thyme and marjoram and water well.

3 potted plants

Most vegetables will grow well in pots, even small containers. Place stones or broken pot pieces in the bottom of the pot and fill with a good, fresh compost. Sow the seed thinly on the top and cover with a thin layer of compost. Cover the pot with netting to prevent birds or other animals from disturbing the compost.

4 strawberry pot

There are several types of strawberry pots available; the most decorative are tall terra-cotta towers that have planting holes in the sides as well as on top. Strawberry towers are also available in plastic.

5 irrigation pipe

Tall strawberry pots are difficult to water right to the bottom, but it is easy to make a simple device to ensure they are well irrigated. Buy a length of 2 in (5 cm) diameter plastic pipe (drainpipe will do). Drill three $1/8$ in (3 mm) holes around the pipe at 2 in (5 cm) intervals along its length.

6 making up the pot

Place the pipe in the center of the pot and fill around it with compost until you reach the first hole in the side of the pot. Place the strawberry roots through the hole and continue to fill with compost until the next hole is reached. Plant further strawberries until the pot is filled.

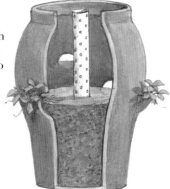

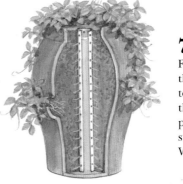

7 watering the strawberry pot

Fill up the pipe with water, and water the top of the pot. If the bottom of the tube is not in tight contact with the bottom of the pot, the water may run out too quickly. If this is the case, slow down its release by ramming a ball of crumpled polyethylene down the tube. This will slow the flow sufficiently to allow water to percolate out of the side holes. Water the pot regularly so that it never dries out.

8 care and maintenance

Water the pots every day and feed with a liquid feed once a week. Keep the plants neat, removing diseased individuals on sight. Harvest vegetables and fruit as required; avoid leaving over-ripe and rotting produce on the plants.

plant list

1 lemon balm	7 bush tomato	13 leeks
2 rosemary	8 cordon tomato	14 lettuce
3 lemon verbena	9 gooseberry	15 potatoes
4 climbing beans	10 patio rose	16 zucchini
5 sage	11 beets	17 marjoram
6 carrots	12 strawberries	18 pear tree

fruit trees in pots

Fruit is usually associated with large bushes or even huge trees, but most varieties have dwarf forms that grow well in containers; there are even apple trees that can be grown as patio plants. However, it is the more exotic fruit, such as oranges and lemons, that are especially good for using in containers. This is partly because they are easier to look after if they can be moved in and outdoors, but also because their fruit and foliage are very decorative.

materials & equipment

terra-cotta pots
stones for drainage
potting compost
slow-release fertilizer or liquid feed
pruning shears

young fruit trees

1 selecting pots

Pots should be considered from a practical as well as aesthetic perspective. Plastic pots are much lighter than terra-cotta but easier to over-water and provide less thermal insulation for a plant's roots in winter. Terra-cotta pots look better with the Mediterranean fruit trees used here. They are cooler in summer and warmer in winter, and are heavier than plastic, which means that they are less likely to fall over in a wind; however, they are more difficult to move when full of compost.

2 planting the trees

Place stones or broken pot pieces in the bottom of the pots to aid drainage. Partly fill with compost; place the plant in and fill up to the top. Firm down and water.

3 choosing a position

While most exotic fruit trees need winter protection, they can be placed outside during the summer. They are best positioned against a south-facing wall. This not only provides a good backdrop, but also stores heat during the day, providing warmth during cool nights. Placing them in a corner offers even better protection. Avoid locations overshadowed by other buildings or trees, or those that funnel drafts over the trees. Containers should be watered every day, and at least twice on hot days or when there is a drying wind. A liquid feed can be added to the water once a month.

4 repotting

The plants used are all perennials and so need to be repotted every year into larger pots until they reach their maximum size. Remove them from their existing pot and shake off any loose compost around the root ball. As the plants get toward their maximum size, some of the roots can be trimmed back. Repot into a pot one size larger using fresh compost and water well.

5 the fruiting plants

In temperate climates, oranges, lemons, and limes can be grown purely as ornamentals, but they will fruit if given enough warmth. To maximize fruiting in cooler areas, the plants, in their pots, should be kept in a greenhouse or solarium to provide them with extra warmth.

plant list: fruit trees
1 Calamondin orange
   (*Citrofortunella microcarpa*)
2 Natal Plum (*Carissa grandiflora*)
3 Meyer's lemon (*Citrus meyeri* 'Meyer')
4 variegated lemon
   (*Citrus limon* 'Variegata')

additional plants
It is a good idea to have one or two pots of smaller plants to act as fillers around the edge of the group. Climbers provide a back-drop for the arrangement of pots.

5 assorted low-growing ornamentals
6 rosemary (*Rosmarinus officinalis*)
7 wisteria (*Wisteria floribunda*)

6 winter care

Most exotic fruit trees and bushes are not winter hardy and so need to be moved under cover—a warm greenhouse or solarium is ideal. The plants should be kept inside until all possible threat of frost has passed and the daytime temperature reaches an average of 68 °F (20 °C). Be careful not to over-water during the winter—just keep the soil barely moist.

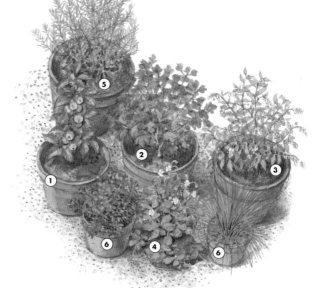

alternative fruit tree arrangement
Less exotic fruits are hardier and can be left outside as long as their containers do not freeze solid. Protect the containers by wrapping straw or bubble wrap around them when cold weather is forecast. Remove the wrapping in warm weather.

1 pole apple
2 standard gooseberry
3 blueberry
4 strawberry tower
5 rosemary
6 additional plants (as above)

chili peppers in pots

Of all vegetables, chili peppers are perhaps the most suitable for growing in pots. They make a spectacular display, as well as providing spice for the kitchen. There is a wide range of varieties available that produce yellow, orange, red, or purple fruit in bushes of different sizes; in some cultivars, the peppers hang from the branches, and in others they are borne upright. Chili peppers grow slowly in temperate climates; the first fruits will appear about fifteen weeks after planting.

materials & equipment

seed trays
sowing compost
3 in (7.5 cm) pots for seedlings
large terra-cotta pots
broken pieces of pot
potting compost
watering can
high-potash liquid feed

chili pepper plants in variety
or
seed of several varieties

1 chili pepper varieties

Chili peppers are branching perennials that can grow to a height of 5 ft (1.5 m). They are sub-tropical plants and will not tolerate frosts or low temperatures. Therefore they must be started off in a greenhouse or solarium and not placed outside until the threat of frost has passed. The different varieties of chili peppers vary in size and shape. They start green but redden as they ripen. The riper they are, the hotter they become.

2 growing from seed

If you cannot obtain young plants, chili peppers may be grown from seed, which is more readily available. Sow the seed in trays in early- to mid-spring and place in a warm place or propagator at about 70 °F (21 °CF). Don't let the seed dry out. If in a propagator, there should be no need to water.

3 potting the seedlings

When large enough to handle, move the plants out into individual pots and continue to grow in a warm environment. Avoid placing the pots in a cold draft and beware of frost.

4 containers

Terra-cotta pots are perfect for growing peppers; ideally, use pots that are less than about 18 in (45 cm) across because they are light enough to be moved inside during cooler weather. The pots must have a hole in the bottom to allow excess water to drain away.

5 repotting

Once the plants are about 4 in (10 cm) high, plant them into their final pots. Cover the bottom of the pot with stones or broken pot; fill with a good quality compost and plant the chili. Water well. If using large pots, place them in their final position before filling with compost; moist compost adds greatly to the weight.

6 pinching out

When the plants reach a height of about 6 in (15 cm), pinch off their growing tops to make them bush out. Chili peppers need a sheltered site and should be placed against a south-facing wall, which will radiate heat during the night, helping to keep the plants warm. Plants should be taken indoors if the temperature drops below 65 °F (18 °C). Sweet peppers will tolerate slightly cooler conditions and can be used as a substitute.

7 displaying, watering, and feeding

If the plants you have chosen are about the same height, use some form of staging—such as bricks or inverted pots—to vary the level. This will display the plants to best effect and let light through to the plants at the back. The plants will need watering every day and perhaps twice a day in very hot weather. High-potash liquid feed should be added to the water every ten days once the fruit has started to swell.

8 harvesting

The pepper can be picked as soon as it is large enough. It can be picked at the green stage when it will be at its mildest or at its final colored stage (red, yellow, or purple) when it will be hotter. Pick the pepper with part of the stalk still attached. Be certain to have picked all the peppers, or have moved the plants inside, before the first frost.

right Grape vines are decorative, productive, and can help utilize space in the garden that would otherwise go unfilled. Vines are also useful for covering eyesores such as garages and oil storage tanks.

above Pears, like most other fruit trees, can be trained in ways to suit the small garden. Full-size trees may be out of the question, but cordons, for example, take up very little space.

below Although hops are perennials, they die back to the ground each year. These dense, twining plants are perfect for growing up trellis to create a backdrop to the vegetable garden.

climbing fruit and vegetables

Many people see the vegetable garden as a flat, utilitarian area of planting, but a far more interesting scene can be created by adding height to the beds using permanent objects, such as fruit trees grown against walls or forming walkways, or other decorative features. Climbing annuals, including climbing beans and trailing zucchini, can also be used to great effect. They can be grown up temporary supports, such as cane tepees, or trail over more permanent structures, such as a metal archways or arbors. Carefully chosen, the structures themselves can add vertical interest to the garden throughout the year.

above Apples and pears can be trained in many ways. A decorative method suitable for use in the kitchen garden is to train them over iron frameworks to form walkways or arbors.

below Grape vines need not be grown in a controlled manner on conventional wirework. They can be allowed to ramble over arches to make shady paths and sitting areas.

below Beans provide a strong vertical element in the kitchen garden. They can be grown up a variety of frameworks, including rows or tepees of canes, or poles, strings, or netting.

below Cordon tomatoes can be trained up canes in the main beds or supported by fences. While bush tomatoes are more practical because they do not need staking, they are not as attractive.

57

pear tunnel

A pergola or archway covered with pears is a romantic addition to the
garden, which provides a good crop as well as decorative interest
throughout the year. In the winter there is the tracery of the bare
branches to be admired. In spring, pure white blossom covers
the arches. In the heat of summer the leaves provide a cool, shady
walkway. In autumn there is, of course, the fruit to be enjoyed
and, finally, the blaze of color as the foliage takes on its autumn
tints before dropping.

materials & equipment

custom-made steel pergola
galvanized wire
2 turnbuckles per horizontal wire
bolts to connect the tops of the curved metal uprights
pegs and string
$^3/_4$-in stone
builder's sand
cement
gravel
3 x $^1/_2$ in (7. 5 x 1 cm) edging boards
plant ties

spade
shovel
wrench to fit turnbuckles
wrench to fit bolts on uprights
garden roller
pruning shears

2 maiden whip pear trees per 18 in (45 cm) of tunnel
well-rotted organic material

1 choosing a framework

Tunnels for carrying fruit trees are available by mail order or from nurseries, but it's best to have one made to your specifications by a workshop. The simplest tunnel is no more than of a line of metal arches. Each arch is made from two curved posts bolted together at the apex; the posts have holes along their length through which wires can be run. Here, the posts are steel, about 1/4 in (6 mm) thick and 2 in (4 cm) wide.

2 laying out the plan

When planning the tunnel, don't forget that the branches and fruit will hang down within, so allow plenty of space to walk through. Lay out the plan of the walkway, marking the position of the leg of each arch with pegs set 3 ft (90 cm) apart. Use shorter pegs and string to mark the path and beds to be planted.

3 securing the posts

Dig a hole 18–24 in (45–60 cm) deep and about 12 in (30 cm) square for each upright and tip in about 5 in (13 cm) of 3/4-in stone. Place the leg in position and fill the hole with cement. Before the cement sets, check with a level that the post is vertical, and that it meets the opposite side of the arch. Bolt the two halves of the arch together.

4 horizontal supports

When the cement has set, thread galvanized wire through holes in the posts to form horizontal supports. Pull the wire as tight as possible and then connect each end to a turnbuckle. Tighten the turnbuckles so that the wires have no slack left in them.

5 laying a path

To lay a gravel path through the tunnel, first excavate the area to a depth of 8 in (20 cm). Lay treated edging boards around the perimeter of the dug area. Fill with 4 in (10 cm) of 3/4-in stone and cover with 2 in (5 cm) of sand. Compact the sand with a roller and top up with 1–2 in (3–5 cm) of gravel, rolling it in several layers.

6 planting the pear trees

Plant the trees at 18 in (45 cm) intervals. At each planting site, thoroughly dig the soil and add as much well-rotted compost as possible. The best time for planting is in early spring. Set the plants in the ground so that the top of the rootball is level with the surface of the soil. Firm them in and water.

7 pruning

When planted 18 in (45 cm) apart, the trees are trained as cordons (each cordon is basically a single stem with short laterals on each side). Reduce the laterals to about three leaves when planting and cut back any new laterals to the same amount each summer. New growth on old laterals should be pruned back to one leaf.

8 finished arch

After a few years, the leaders will meet at the top of the arch; new growth should then be restricted to one bud. Keep the trees pruned or they will rapidly become overgrown. Harvest the pears as soon as they ripen; they are ready as soon as they come away easily by twisting the fruit.

bean arbor

A seat beneath a flower-laden arbor is a feature associated with formal ornamental gardens, but there is no reason why such a decorative refuge cannot be incorporated into the kitchen garden. Covered with climbing beans, the arbor can be both beautiful and productive. It is possible to create a permanent structure or something more temporary, which can be moved from one year to the next.

materials & equipment

purchased or custom-made arbor framework
pegs and string
¾-in stone
treated edging boards ¾ in (2 cm) deep, 9 in (23 cm) wide,
coarse gravel
sand
pea gravel
cement

spade
shovel
trowel
rake
garden roller
tamper

4 scarlet runner bean plants (*Phaseolus coccineus*) per 3 ft (1 m)
well-rotted organic material

1 selecting an arbor
Choose an arbor frame from a nursery or mail order catalog, or find a blacksmith who will produce a more unusual design to your specifications. Think carefully about size—you may wish to fit a table as well as a bench under the arbor—and you should allow about 12 in (30 cm) for growth of the climbing beans within the frame.

2 preparing the ground
Clear the area of ground on which you want to place the arbor. Peg out the position of the arbor legs, and use further pegs and string to mark out the edges of a seating area and approaching path, both of which will be laid with gravel for durability.

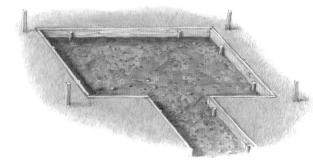

3 excavating the base
In the seating and path area, dig down to a depth of 8 in (20 cm) and remove the soil. Place treated boards around the dug area, securing with wooden pegs at 3 ft (1 m) intervals. Use a heavy roller to flatten the base.

4 laying the path and base
Cover the base of the excavated area with 3/4-in stone to a depth of 4 in (10 cm). Lay a middle layer of coarse gravel and sand 2 in (5 cm) deep, and cover this with 1 in (2.5 cm) of pea gravel. Rake the surface.

5 securing the arbor
In sheltered sites, you don't need to cement in the uprights of the arbor frame. Dig a hole for each post at least 18 in (45 cm) deep. Add a 4 in (10 cm) layer of gravel and place the framework in position. Refill the holes, ramming down the earth firmly with a tamper. In exposed sites, it is best to cement the framework into position because wind pressure on the plant-covered arbor can be significant.

6 planting and watering
After the threat of frost has passed, dig the soil around the arbor and plant the climbing beans. Plant a seedling against each post and then at 10 in (25 cm) intervals. Scatter slug pellets around the base. Water thoroughly.

7 training the beans
Beans will naturally twine up and over the arbor, but it may be necessary to direct them at the initial stages to ensure that there is even coverage. There is no need to tie the stems—it is enough just to tuck them in.

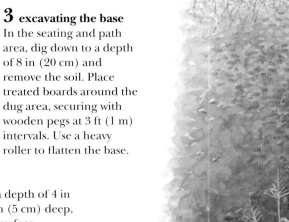

8 arbor in bloom
Don't let the beans dry out, especially once the flowers have started to form. To encourage bushier growth, pinch out the tops of the stems when they reach the middle of the arbor. The beans produce a display of red, pink, or white flowers, depending on variety.

9 harvesting the beans
Pick the beans when about 6 in (15 cm) long. Harvest every three to four days, taking the beans before their seeds swell. Don't leave old pods on the plants; they inhibit the formation of new ones.

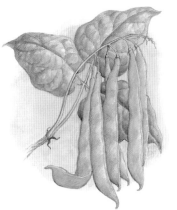

wall-trained red currants

Red currants are a neglected fruit in the garden. This is surprising because they have a deliciously fresh taste that is a treat whether they are eaten from the bush or as part of a dish. Culinary benefits aside, red currants are also very attractive plants. When grown in conventional bushes, they have a certain appealing quality, but they are at their best when trained against a wall. White currants and gooseberries can be grown to spectacular effect in the same way.

materials & equipment

wall plugs
vine eyes and straining bolt
turnbuckle
2 garden canes per plant
plant ties

drill with masonry bit
hammer
pliers
spade and pruning shears

red currant plants
well-rotted organic material

1 supporting the red currant plant

The currant bush will need some form of support against the wall. The best way of securing it, especially if several bushes are to be grown, is to use eye bolts that hammer or screw into the wall, through which galvanized wire is threaded and secured. The wires should be about 18 in (45 cm) apart and the supporting eye bolts at 3 ft (90 cm) intervals.

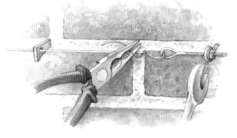

2 fixing the wires

Thread the wire through the eye bolts. Fasten the wire at one end using pliers to twist it back on itself. Use a turnbuckle at the other end to make the wire as taut as possible. Attach the bolt to the wall through an eye bolt.

vine eyes
These galvanized fasteners come in various shapes. Some are nailed into the wall; others screw into wall plugs.

3 choosing a plant

Choose a red currant bush with two strong shoots coming from the rootstock. If there are more, remove the extra ones with a pair of pruning shears, cutting as close to their base as possible. If there is only one main shoot, choose a plant with a strong, low-down side shoot. Thoroughly prepare the ground in which the currant is to be planted by removing any perennial weeds and incorporating plenty of manure.

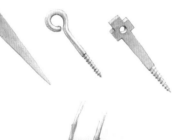

4 planting

Plant the bush a little way out from the wall. It should be at the same depth in the soil as it was in its original container. Fasten two canes vertically to the wires, making paths along which the currant can be trained. Tie in the two main stems, one to each cane. Remove any side shoots back to one bud.

5 pruning

As the two main stems grow, tie them in to the canes, removing any new side shoots back to the first bud. Completely remove any shoots below 10 in (25 cm) on the main stems.

climbing alternatives

three stem cordon
Gooseberries, red currants, and white currants can be grown in three-stemmed cordons. The method is basically the same as described for the double cordon, except that the central, as well as two side shoots, are retained.

fan planting
Currants can be trained into a fan, making a spectacular display against a wall. The best fruits are produced in sunny, sheltered spots, but red currants can thrive against north-facing walls.

6 maintenance and training

Every summer cut back any side shoots to four of five leaves. In the winter reduce these even further, back to one or two buds. Follow these pruning procedures annually to maximize fruit yield. Once the two main leaders have reached the height you want, cut out the tips.

red currant fence
Trained red currants can liven up tired wooden fences, trellising, or even open wirework. Bushes can be grown to a height of 6 ft (2 m), and produce a crop of about 2.2 lb (1 kg) of fruit per year over a period of ten to twelve years.

apple arch

A kitchen garden can be much more than a two-dimensional planting. The best designs make full use of the available area and height to maximize productivity and decorative impact. Certain vegetables, such as climbing beans, add dimension to the garden, but ideally, more permanent features should be incorporated to define the space. An apple arch in the center of the garden where paths meet adds a touch of elegance as well as permanence to the garden.

materials & equipment

purchased arch
or
8 lengths of 11 1/2 ft (3.5 m) x 1/2 in (1 cm) steel rod
4 lengths of 15 ft (4.6 m) x 1/2 in (1 cm) steel rod
8 in (20 cm) length of copper water pipe
3/4-in stone
galvanized wire
paint (metal primer, undercoat, and topcoat)
cement
string or plant ties

spade
shovel
level
two-foot square
hacksaw
pliers
pruning shears

4 feathered-maiden apple trees
well-rotted organic material

1 planning

Arches can be bought from nurseries or mail-order catalogs but it is easy to make one from ^{1}/2 in (1 cm) steel rod usually used for cement reinforcing. When choosing an arch, be generous with size—an arch 6 ^{1}/2 ft (2 m) tall will have a clearance of just 5 ^{1}/2 ft (1.7 m) once covered with the tree. First, use pegs to mark the positions of the arch's legs in the corners of a plot 7 x 7 ft (2.2 x 2.2 m). Use a two-foot square and strings to check that it is square.

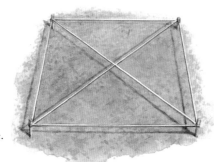

2 home-made framework

Each of the four legs of the arch is made from three steel rods. Using a hacksaw, cut two 11 ^{1}/2 ft (3.5 m) lengths and one 15 ft (4.6 m) length. Bind the three rods together with wire up to a height of 6 ft (1.8 m) so that they form a single column.

3 preparing the foundations

At the foot of each of the four legs, dig a hole 18 in (45 cm) deep and 12 in (30 cm) wide. Ram ^{3}/4-in stone into the base to a depth of about 4 in (10 cm).

4 setting in the legs

Place each leg into a dug hole. Carefully check that the leg is upright using a spirit level. Fill the hole with cement to set in the legs. Ensure that the long steel rod of each leg faces into the middle of the arch before pouring the cement and allowing it to set.

5 forming the arches

Once the cement has set, bend each rod over to meet its opposite number. Try to keep the curves as even as possible. The short rods bend to make the perimeter of the arch, while the long rods bend to meet in the middle of the arch to form its "roof."

6 securing the arches

Where two rods meet, they can either be bound with wire or secured by using an 8 in (20 cm) length of copper water pipe as a sleeve to hold them together. The rods may need to be cut to their final length with a hacksaw before the sleeve is fitted.

7 completing the structure

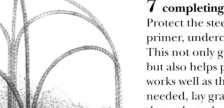

Protect the steel rods by applying a metal primer, undercoat, and a topcoat of paint. This not only gives the frame a good finish but also helps prevent rusting. The arch works well as the centerpiece of a garden; if needed, lay gravel paths running through the arch, as described on page 59.

8 planting

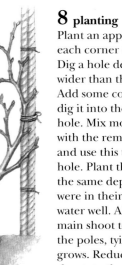

Plant an apple tree at each corner of the arch. Dig a hole deeper and wider than the rootball. Add some compost and dig it into the base of the hole. Mix more compost with the remaining soil and use this to refill the hole. Plant the trees at the same depth as they were in their pots and water well. Allow the main shoot to grow up the poles, tying in as it grows. Reduce the side shoots to three leaves or three buds.

9 training side shoots

When the main stem grows past the point where the legs divide, allow two side shoots to develop, tying them in as they grow. Again reduce any new side shoots to three leaves and cut back material on older growth to one leaf.

10 maintenance

Prune in winter and summer, cutting back any new side shoots to three leaves, while pruning the new growth on older material back to one leaf. Pick the fruit when ripe for eating, or when firm but just under-ripe for storage. Wrap each fruit in waxed paper and store in a well-ventilated container in a cool, dark place.

decorative beds and borders

While the main purpose of a kitchen garden is to provide tasty produce for year-round use at the table, it is easy to create a plot that will satisfy the eye as well as the palette. Evergreen herbs can be used to provide interest across the seasons, and many vegetables, such as Swiss chard, with its brilliant red stems, are just as comfortable in a flower border as in a vegetable patch. Old-fashioned kitchen gardens often contained flowers, including pot marigolds, which can still be used to add points of bright color to the garden.

above Lettuces are available in a huge range of leaf shapes and colors. Frilly-leaved and red-hued varieties are particularly attractive. Spring onions provide a contrasting leaf-shape in the salad bed.

right The sages, *Salvia officinalis*, are useful herbs in the kitchen. 'Purpurascens' mixes well with ornamental plants. It is seen here with the silver-leaved lamb's ears (*Stachys byzantina*).

below Fruit trees have several decorative phases. Leaf burst is a welcome sign of spring; in summer their shapes provide vertical interest; and in autumn there is fruit and colorful foliage to enjoy.

above Shrubby herbs, such as this perennial, evergreen sage *Salvia officinalis* 'Icterina', provide a backbone to the decorative kitchen garden.

below Flowers, such as pot marigolds (*Calendula officinalis*) also find use in the kitchen. Their petals can be added to salads or used as a substitute for saffron.

above Fruit trees provide a very decorative element in any kitchen garden. They can be used as standard trees or bushes, but become even more interesting when trained over metal frameworks to become archways, walkways, or even low hedges.

below A potager is, strictly speaking, simply a kitchen garden, but the term is increasingly used to describe an ordered, decorative plot that also provides food for the kitchen. Here fruit trees, scented flowers, paths, and, of course, vegetables are combined to stunning effect.

fruit among the flowers

Fruit trees and bushes are permanent features in the garden. When in blossom or fruit they are very decorative in their own right, and if trained as standards they add a sculptural quality to the garden. At some times of the year they may become a bit dull, but the plot can be brightened up by planting flowers around their bases to create a scene that changes throughout the seasons.

materials & equipment

spade
fork
rake
trowel
garden line or pegs and string
pruning shears

2 standard gooseberry bushes
corn marigold (*Chrysanthemum segetum*) seed
love-in-a-mist (*Nigella damascena*) seed
1 *Geranium endressii*
6 box plants (*Buxus sempervirens* 'Suffruticosa') per 3 ft (1 m) of hedging

1 planning
Fruit trees and bushes take several years to mature, so any mistakes you make in the design will be difficult to rectify. Carefully plan your planting scheme on paper before transferring it to the ground. Use a grid of canes and strings to help with the layout on the ground if necessary.

2 the hedge
Planting a box hedge (see page 23) around the plot makes it a self-contained entity and helps neaten the bed by preventing plants from flopping onto the adjacent path. Use a garden line to ensure that the hedge is planted in a straight line. When mature, it should be trimmed at least once a year.

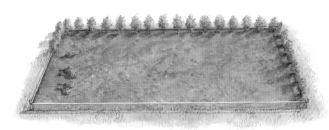

3 the standard gooseberries
Gooseberry bushes can be bought ready-trained into standards, but it is cheaper and more fun to train your own. This is done by grafting the chosen fruiting variety on to *Ribes odoratum* rootstock. Buy and plant a *Ribes odoratum*. Mulch with well-rotted manure. Select one stem to train vertically and prune back the lateral branches. The plant will be ready to accept a graft in about three years.

4 under-planting
Both annuals and perennials can be planted around the growing gooseberry bushes. Corn marigolds, which are self-sowing (and so save time and energy), work particularly well when mixed with love-in-a-mist and perennial geraniums. The latter should be cut to the ground after flowering to encourage a late flush of foliage and some late flowers.

5 grafting the gooseberry
After three years, the gooseberry rootstock will have grown to about 3 ft (1 m). Take a cutting of, or buy, the desired scion variety. Trim all the side shoots from the rootstock and graft the two together using the whip and tongue technique.

6 binding
Unite scion and rootstock, trying not to touch the cut surfaces of either. Bind the two together with clear polythene tape. Remove the tape very carefully when the join between scion and rootstock begins to form a callus.

7 securing and pruning the bushes
By the next season, the gooseberry graft should have formed a normal spreading bush on top of the *R. odoratum* stem. Use a thick stake and tree tie to secure the bush. Prune the bush as you would a normal established gooseberry or red currant (see page 68).

8 the mature bed
Under-planting can be varied from year to year or even within a year. Pansies that give late season color can be followed by spring bedding, such as forget-me-nots. A range of plants can be used in the summer by sowing direct onto the soil or planting out.

decorative vegetable garden

In many modern potagers, the planting is so regimented that harvesting just a single lettuce leaves a gap that spoils the appearance of the whole plot. But it is possible to create a more practical working garden that is highly decorative and yet is not a slave to precision planting. The attractions of this garden come from its overall composition and surroundings; indeed, much interest is generated by the irregularity and variation of the crops.

materials & equipment

280 bricks
36 paving slabs 2 x 2 ft (60 x 60 cm)
16 trellis panels 6 x 6 ft (1.8 x 1.8 m)
2 trellis panels 3 x 6 ft (90 cm x 1.8 m)
20 treated wooden posts 4 in x 4 in x 8 ft (10 cm x 10 cm x 2.5 m)
galvanized nails
2 cu yd (2 cu m) sand
7 cu ft (0.2 cu m) ³⁄4-in stone
1 cu yd (1 cu m) concrete
decorative urn
12 garden canes 8 ft (2.5 m) long

spade, fork and trowel
tamper
saw and hammer
level
wheelbarrow
garden line or pegs and string

seed and plants in variety

1 planning

Carrying out the hard landscaping is a major task that needs careful planning. First draw up all the elements on squared paper—this will make it easier to transfer your plan to the ground. At this stage, also draw up a plant list to help ensure that you can get the seedlings or seeds in good time.

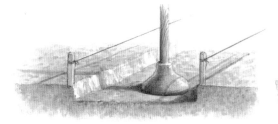

2 preparing the ground

Use pegs and string to mark out the position of the paving and bricks to be laid on the ground. The slabs do not need to be set in cement; simply ram down the earth within the marked lines as firmly as possible with a tamper.

3 laying the paving

Put down a layer of sand 1–2 in (2.5–5 cm) deep and set the slabs and brick on this, making certain that they are level and firm. Plain, natural-colored paving slabs look best in a vegetable garden.

4 erecting the trellising

The plot is surrounded by rustic trellising on which decorative climbers and fruiting trees are grown. To ensure that the trellis is secure enough to take the considerable load, especially when the wind is blowing, the uprights should be cemented in the ground. The panels can be nailed or screwed to the uprights. Treat the uprights and the trellis panels with a plant-friendly wood preservative.

5 planting the hop

Hops are highly decorative plants to grow on the trellises; they are of practical use only if you brew your own beer. When buying, ensure that you have a female plant because the male does not bear fruit. Plant at the same depth as it was in the pot. In spring, spread the young shoots out along the trellis so that the plant covers a wide area. In autumn, cut right back to the ground and remove all the old growth.

6 bean tepee

Climbing beans can be grown up a conventional bean fence or in a tepee, which takes up less space. Push 8 ft (2.5 m) canes or poles into the ground so that their bases form a circle. The bases of the canes should be about 12 in (30 cm) apart. They should all be sloped slightly toward the center of the circle so that the tops all meet. Bundle the tops together and tie tightly with string.

7 planting

The planting can be changed from year to year; for the best effect, mix plants that you use most in the kitchen with some ornamentals. The design of the garden benefits from sparing use of architectural features—here a stone urn.

the plants

1 vine	**7** ornamental kale	**13** leeks
2 hops	**8** beets	**14** endive
3 cordon apples	**9** parsley	**15** parsnips
4 spinach	**10** climbing beans	**16** tomatoes
5 carrots	**11** chives	
6 lettuce	**12** zucchini	

step-over apple hedge

Gone are the days when growing apples meant large trees taking up precious areas of garden space. Now they can be grown in all kinds of innovative ways suitable for the smaller garden. The step-over hedge is an excellent example. Here, an apple tree is trained as two horizontal branches only a short way above the ground. Growing the tree is not difficult—in essence it is training an apple tree as an espalier with just one horizontal tier—but it does require patience.

materials & equipment

One 30 in (75 cm) metal or wooden post per 6 ft (2 m) length of hedge
galvanized wire
4 garden canes per tree
plant ties

spade
hammer
drill
pruning shears

1 maiden whip apple tree per 12 ft (4 m) length of hedge
well-rotted organic material

1 planning the plot
Decide where you are going to put the trees and draw a plan to scale so that you can work out how many you will need and how much space they will take up. The distance between trees will vary depending on variety and stock, but they will usually extend at least 6 ft (2 m) on either side of the main stem when mature.

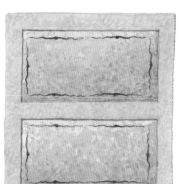

7 lowering the canes
In the winter of the first year, gently pull down the canes and tie them to the horizontal wires. Cut back both main shoots by about a third to a downward facing bud. Any shoots that have grown off the main horizontals should be cut down to three or four buds.

2 preparing the ground
Use pegs to mark out the planting sites on the ground and thoroughly prepare the ground in each position. Double-dig the ground, working in plenty of well-rotted organic material.

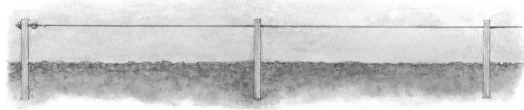

8 summer pruning
Continue to prune as described above during the summer and winter of each year, allowing the horizontal shoots to grow longer until they have reached a length of about 6 ft (2 m). Cut back new side shoots to three or four buds and reduce new growth on existing side shoots to one leaf bud.

3 supporting the hedge
The apple hedge can usually support its own weight when mature. Before this, it must be held up by wires stretched taut between posts. Wooden posts are acceptable, since by the time they have rotted they are no longer needed. Metal posts can also be used, giving support even when the tree is mature. Whether wooden or metal, posts should be knocked into the ground at 6 ft (2 m) intervals; the wire stretched between them should be about 12 in (30 cm) from the ground.

4 stretching the wire
Use tensioning bolts to pull the horizontal wires tight. Twist the wire through the loop of the bolt and tighten the nut to tension.

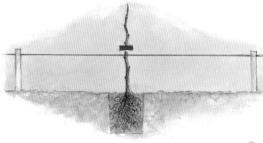

5 planting
Plant the young apple trees at their marked positions to the same depth as they were in their pots (or nursery beds if bare rooted). Cut off the leader just above the wire, ensuring that there are two buds roughly level with, or just below, the wire.

6 support for growing shoots
Tie two canes to the wire; angle them at about 45° using further canes to support their tops. As the two shoots grow, tie them to the canes. Remove any other shoots that may appear below.

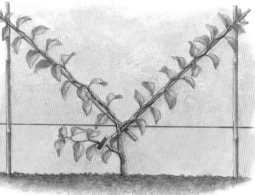

9 harvesting
The time for harvesting will depend on the variety used. As a rule of thumb, apples are usually ripe when they come away in the hand when gently twisted. Early varieties do not store, but later ones can be kept for several months in a cool place. Check periodically than none have rotted.

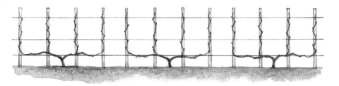

tall hedge
A higher apple hedge can be created by pruning several trees into multiple-stem cordons. Again, after a few years they will no longer require wire supports. Mature trees resemble a row of candelabras.

herb border

Herb gardens need a surprising amount of upkeep, and there are times of the year—especially from late summer onward—when they begin to look a bit tired. One solution is to grow the herbs among other flowers in a mixed border. When in season, the herbs add their fragrance and charm to the border; other plants take over when the herbs are not at their best. Another benefit of a mixed planting is that herbs can be harvested when ready without leaving conspicuous gaps in the garden.

materials & equipment

$^1/_2$ x 4 in (1 x 10 cm) edging board
$^1/_2$ x 1 $^3/_4$ in (1 x 4 cm) pegs
stepping stones or broken slabs
1 x 8 ft (30 cm x 2.4 m) heavy-duty polyethylene sheet

spade
fork
rake
trowel
hammer
tamper

herbs and decorative plants in variety
well-rotted organic material

1 planning the border
Carefully draw out a plan of the permanent features of the herb garden. Be sure to allow access to all parts of the plot from a central gravel path by planning in stepping stones. These can be square, circular, or irregular paving slabs; they do not need to be cemented in place and so can be moved if the planting is changed. The plot shown here measures 8 x 8 ft (2.4 m x 2.4 m).

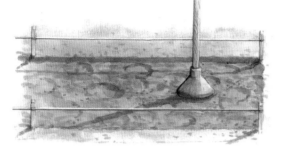

2 preparing the ground
Use pegs and string to mark out the position of the path on the ground. Tamp down the soil firmly, so that the gravel will be almost flush to the ground when laid. Also tamp down the soil where the stepping stones are to be laid.

3 making the path edging
To prevent the gravel spilling into the border, construct a simple edging strip from lengths of ¹/₂ x 4 in (1 x 10 cm) treated timber. For every 3 ft (90 cm) of edging board, nail in a 6 in (15 cm) upright that has been sharpened to form a peg.

4 filling the path
Gently hammer the pegs (and edging board) into the ground along the line of the path. Line the floor of the path with heavy-duty polyethylene before pouring in the gravel—this will help suppress weed growth. Fill the prepared path with a 4 in (10 cm) depth of gravel and rake the surface.

5 laying the stepping stones
When laying the paving slabs, bed them onto a 2 in (5 cm) layer of sand to make them level.

6 preparing and planting
Dig over the bed in autumn, removing any perennial weeds and adding well-rotted organic material. In spring, rake it through, removing any new weeds that have appeared. Place the plants, still in their pots, in position on the border. Stand back and try to envision them in full growth, making any necessary adjustments to their positions. Mix the plants so that the herbs are scattered throughout the border. This not only masks them during their less interesting phases but also means that you can savor their individual fragrances more easily. Plant out, starting from the back of the plot. Water well. Rake over the border to even the soil and remove footprints. If you intend to mulch, do so now.

7 confining the mint
The mint and the white willowherb are both runners and are best confined to prevent their spreading over the other plants. Small areas can be controlled by planting in a bottomless bucket. Larger confined areas can be created by digging a trench around the planting and inserting a vertical layer of thick polythene, at least 12 in (30 cm) deep.

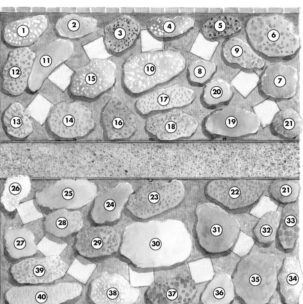

8 the complete plan
Draw up a complete planting plan. It is important not to underestimate the size to which some plants will grow. The plan is not sacrosanct and plants can change from year to year.

9 care and maintenance
Herb gardens tend to become messy if not given regular attention. Deadhead flowering stems unless seed is required, and remove all vegetation that is dying back or already dead.

plant list
1 *Philadelphus* 'Sybille' (mock orange) x 1
2 *Foeniculum vulgare* (fennel) x 3
3 *Lathyrus odoratus* (sweet peas) x 8
4 *Angelica archangelica*
5 *Oenothera biennis* (evening primrose) x 3
6 *Cynara cardunculus* (cardoon) x 1
7 *Satureja montana* (winter savory) x 1
8 *Petroselinum crispum* (parsley) x 5
9 *Borago officinalis* (borage) x 3
10 *Epilobium angustifolium* 'Album' (willowherb) x 3
11 *Mentha spicata* (mint) x 3
12 *Aster x frikartii* x 1
13 *Lavandula stoechas pedunculata* x 1
14 *Nepeta x faasinnii* (catmint) x 2
15 *Allium tuberosum* (garlic chives) x 5
16 *Achillea millefolium* 'Cerise Queen' (yarrow) x 1
17 *Nepeta govaniana* x 3
18 *Lavandula angustifolia* (lavender) x 1
19 *Astrantia major* x 3
20 *Melissa officinalis* (lemon balm) x 1
21 *Laurus nobilis* (bay) x 2
22 *Thymus serpyllum* (thyme) x 3
23 *Nepeta sibrica* x 3
24 *Artemisia dracunculus* (French tarragon) x 3
25 *Origanum vulgare* (oregano) x 3
26 *Tanecetum parthenium* 'Aureum' x 2
27 *Ruta graveolens* (rue) x 1
28 *Calaminta grandiflora* (Calamint) x 1
29 *Iris foetidissima* x 1
30 *Salvia officinalis* 'Icterina' (sage) x 1
31 *Levisticum officinale* (lovage) x 1
32 *Anemone x hybrida* x 3
33 *Allium schoenoprasum* (chives) x 5
34 *Myrrhis odorata* (sweet Cicely) x 1
35 *Rosmarinus officinalis* (rosemary) x 1
36 *Pelargonium graveolens* (scented geranium) x 3
37 *Geranium phaeum* x 1
38 *Dianthus* 'Miss Sinkins' x 3
39 *Alchemilla mollis* (lady's mantle) x 3
40 *Althaea officinalis* (marsh mallow) x 1

vegetables among the flowers

In many traditional cottage gardens, little differentiation was made between flowers, fruit, and vegetables—the three were allowed to blend together organically or actually mixed when planting. Some vegetables can be as decorative as flowering plants, and there is every reason to use them together when designing a garden. Mixing species in this way also offers some protection against the rapid proliferation of a particular pest or disease, which can occur in large stands of a single crop.

materials & equipment

8 treated wooded posts 3 in x 3 in x 4 ft (8 cm x 8 cm x 1.2 m)
8 metal post supports to fit
stout galvanized wire
galvanized staples

sledge hammer
hammer
wire cutter
spade
fork
rake
pruning shears

seed and plants in variety
well-rotted organic material

1 planning
Cottage gardens often seem randomly planted, but careful planning is called for to achieve this look. The garden contains permanent features, such as trees and fences, semi-permanent perennial flowering plants, as well as annuals and bedding plants. To help your planning, sketch out the plot using different blocks of color for trees (blue), espalier trees (green), permanent planting (red), and vegetables and annuals (yellow).

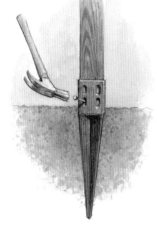

2 fixing the posts
In this garden, two parallel fences support the espalier-trained pears and apples. Ready-made fences of metal uprights and thin metal cross-members are attractive but expensive; wire fences supported by four well-anchored wooden uprights will do the job just as well. Instead of digging holes for the wooden fence posts, use metal post supports. Drive them into the ground with a heavy sledge hammer. It helps to place a piece of wood between post and hammer. Insert the wooden fence posts into the supports. Secure them by nailing through the holes at the base of the metal supports.

3 securing the cross wires
Stretch one length of galvanized wire horizontally across the faces of the four fence posts about 18 in (45 cm) above ground level. Secure with staples hammered into the wood. Strain the wire as tight as you can. Bend back the wire on the end posts and secure with a second staple to ensure that it does not work loose.

4 finishing the fence
Add two more horizontal wires at 12 in (30 cm) intervals above the lowest wire. Erect a second fence of four posts parallel to the first. The posts should be treated with a plant-friendly wood preservative.

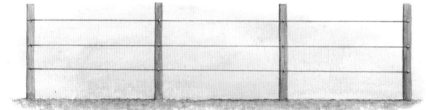

5 espalier apples and pears
In early spring, plant two whip apple trees against one fence, and two whip pears against the other. Secure a cane vertically to the wires using plant ties. Use this to support the whip. After planting, cut the whip back to just above the lowest wire just above a bud that has two strong buds below.

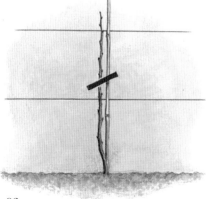

6 training
In summer, select two strong lateral shoots and secure them to canes tied in to the fence at 45° to the upright. Remove any other side shoots back to a couple of leaves; once the main first tier has become established these should be removed altogether, cutting them back flush to the trunk.

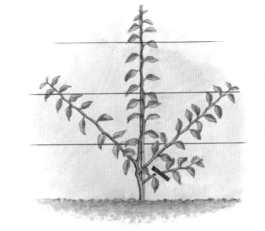

7 pruning
In the first winter, lower the lateral canes to a horizontal position to form the first tier of the espalier. Next, cut the vertical leader to just above the second wire—again, cut just above a bud that has two strong buds below. Repeat the steps above to form the next tiers of the espalier in the following two years.

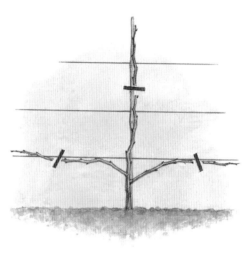

8 perennials
Plant the perennials in the prepared ground in spring at the same depth as they were in their pots. Do not plant them too close together because they will expand into clumps as they grow.

plant list
1 *Helianthus annuus*
2 *Crocosmia* 'Lucifer' x 20
3 *Anthemis* 'Sauce Hollandaise' x 3
4 *Anthemis tinctoria* x 5
5 *x Solidaster luteus* x 2
6 *Hemerocallis* 'Stafford' x 3
7 *Kniphofia* 'Yellow Hammer' x 5
8 apple bush trees in variety
9 whip apple trees for espaliers x 2
10 whip pears for espaliers x 2
11 leeks
12 parsnips
13 Swiss chard
14 spinach

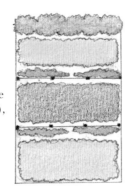

9 other planting
Sow and plant out the vegetables in small irregular blocks according to the instructions on the packets.

plant directory

A NOTE ON LATIN NAMES

Latin names are very rarely given on seed packets of fruit and vegetables; these are almost always sold by their common names. Herbs are usually referred to by their common names, although Latin names sometimes occur, while ornamentals are most frequently identified by their Latin name. Plants in this directory are listed according to these conventions.

VEGETABLES

Nearly all vegetables need an open, sunny position, away from overhanging foliage. In exposed areas, they should be protected from strong winds by using wind-break netting or surrounding the beds with fences or taller hedges of box or similar plants. The best soil for vegetables is a friable loam, either neutral or slightly acid, but they can be grown with success in most other types of soil except those of extreme acidity or alkalinity. Whatever the soil, it can usually be improved by the regular addition of organic material, such as compost or farmyard manure. Even the heaviest clay will eventually succumb to such treatment.

Dig the soil over in the autumn so that it is open to the winter weather, which will help break it down to a fine tilth. Remove any weeds and add plenty of well-rotted organic material. When digging for the first time, it is best to double-dig—that is, to loosen the soil at the bottom of the trench that you are digging. However, avoid mixing this subsoil with the top soil. Check for any weeds that have regenerated before planting in spring. Do not sow or plant out too early. For hardy crops, wait until the soil has warmed up before sowing. Carrots, for example, will not germinate until the soil temperature is at least 45 °F (7 °C). Seed sown before this temperature is reached is liable to rot in the cold, damp soil. Tender crops, such as zucchini and many of the beans, should not be planted outdoors or sown before all threat of frost has passed or they could be killed.

Most vegetables can be sown directly where they are to grow, but it is sometimes more convenient or speedy to germinate them in pots or modules under glass and plant out when they are large enough. A few vegetables, including celery, celeriac, and tomatoes, should always be started off under glass to ensure they grow fast enough to crop before the autumn. Do not plant too close together—always allow room for the plants to develop.

Keep crops weed-free and well watered. Organic or plastic mulch can be applied between plants to help suppress weeds and conserve moisture. Keep an eye out for pests and diseases and take appropriate action. Remember that a kitchen garden with healthy plants is less prone to attack than one in which the plants are neglected.

Taller plants, such as beans and peas, may need support. Leafy ones such as lettuces and cabbages may need protection from birds, and most will need to be protected from slugs; wandering around the

garden at night with a flashlight collecting slugs is enough to keep populations down.

Harvest vegetables as they ripen or as they are required for the table. Details for individual crops are given below. Some can be stored, while others, particularly root crops and some brassicas, such as brussels sprouts, can be left in the ground as long as the weather does not get so cold that the ground freezes. If very cold weather threatens, lift the root vegetables and store them inside.

In the listing below, the term "annual" refers to vegetables that complete their cycle within twelve months, although many are, in fact, biennials or tender perennials. The "recommended" varieties of seed are included for guidance only. They have been chosen for their flavor and decorative qualities. They are all available through mail order catalogs and via the Internet.

artichoke
Hardy perennial. Plant in spring at 30 in (75 cm) intervals in rows set 4 ft (1.2 m) apart. Harvest the flower buds in summer before they open. Best eaten fresh, although "hearts" can be frozen. Recommended variety: 'Vert de Laon'.

asparagus
Hardy perennial. Planted in spring at 12–15 in (30–38 cm) intervals in rows 3 ft (90 cm) apart. The spears or shoots are harvested from late spring to early summer. Can be grown from seed sown in the spring. Best eaten fresh but can be stored by freezing. Recommended variety: 'Lucullus'.

beet
Hardy annual. Grown from seed sown where it is to grow in spring and thinned to 3–4 in (7.5–10 cm) intervals. Rows should be 12 in (30 cm) apart. Best when eaten small, no more than about 3 in (8 cm) across. Can be left in ground until required.
Recommended varieties: 'Albina Vereduna' (white flesh), 'Boltardy', 'Burpees Golden' (yellow flesh), 'Monogram'.

broccoli
Hardy annual. Grown from seed either sown in trays or *in situ*. Plant or thin to 24 in (60 cm) intervals in rows 24 in (60 cm) apart in early summer. Harvest leaves in spring. Best used fresh but can be frozen. Recommended varieties: 'Minaret', 'Nine Star Perennial', 'Purple Sprouting'.

brussels sprout
Hardy annual. Grown from seed sown in seed bed in spring and transplanted when big enough. Plant at 20–30 in (50–75 cm) intervals in rows 30 in (75 cm) apart. Harvest late autumn onward. Can be left on plant until required. Best used fresh but can be frozen. Recommended varieties: 'Bedford Fillbasket', 'Icarus', 'Peer Gynt', 'Rampart'.

bush bean
Tender annual. Sow *in situ* from late spring onward. Thin to 4 in (10 cm) in rows set 18 in (45 cm) apart. Harvest from summer onward. Treat climbing varieties in the same manner as scarlet runners (see page 101). Best used fresh but can be frozen. Recommended varieties: 'Annabel', 'Vilbel'.

cabbage
Hardy annual. Grown from seed sown in seed bed or under glass. Sow from spring to summer depending on variety. Plant at 20–30 in (50–75 cm) intervals in rows 30 in (75 cm) apart. Harvest throughout the year depending on variety. Pick as required. Recommended varieties: 'Ruby Ball' (red cabbage), 'Ice Queen' (Savoy cabbage), 'First Early Market' (spring cabbage), 'Hispi', 'Duncan' (summer cabbages).

calabrese
Hardy annual. Can be sown in modules but best where they are to grow and thinned in late spring. Thin to or plant at 18 in (45 cm) intervals with the same distance between rows. Harvest autumn onward. Best used fresh but can be frozen. Recommended varieties: 'Mercedes', 'Shogun'.

carrot
Hardy annual. Sow very thinly where they are to grow from spring onward. Thin to 3 in (8 cm) in rows set 8–10 in (20–25 cm) apart. Harvest when big enough. Can be left in ground until required or stored in trays of just-moist sand in frost-free position. Recommended varieties: 'Fly Away', 'Nanco'.

cauliflower
Hardy annual. Sow in seed bed in early spring for autumn varieties and early summer for winter varieties. Plant out at 20–30 in (50–75 cm) intervals in rows set 30 in (75 cm) apart. Harvest autumn onward. Can be stored in a cool place for several weeks. Recommended varieties: 'Aubade', 'Kestrel', White Rock'.

celeriac
Tender annual. Sow in trays under glass in spring. Plant out after frosts at 12 in (30 cm) intervals in rows set 16 in (40 cm) apart. Keep well watered. Harvest autumn onward. Can be left in ground until required or stored in trays of just-moist sand in frost-free position. Recommended variety: 'Monarch'.

celery
Tender annual. Sow in trays under glass in spring. Plant out after frosts at 9–12 in (23–30 cm) intervals in rows set 12 in (30 cm) apart. Keep watered. Tie cardboard collars around the stems and earth up to blanch. Harvest autumn onward. Leave in the ground until required. Recommended varieties: 'Giant Pink', 'Ivory Tower'.

chicory
Hardy biennial. Some are grown and used like lettuce; others (witloof) are forced to produce "chicons," blanched shoots of tightly packed leaves. Sow in spring or early summer. Witloof is lifted in autumn; the roots are placed in pots of compost and covered with a light-proof pot. The chicons are harvested as required. Recommended varieties: 'Witloof Zoom' (witloof), 'Red Treviso' (leaf chicory).

chili pepper
Tender annual. Sow in spring under glass; grow under glass except in warm areas. Plant 18–24 in (45–60 cm) apart if grown in the open, closer if in pots. Harvest green or when ripe. Can be dried. Recommended varieties: 'Apache', 'Hot Gold Spike'.

corn
Tender annual. Sow under glass in spring and plant out when frosts have passed. Plant in a block at 12 in (30 cm) intervals each way. Harvest after tassels have withered and cob is plump. Can be frozen. Recommended varieties: 'Sundance', 'Kelvedon Glory'.

cucumber
Tender annual. Sow in spring under glass. Either grow under glass climbing up strings, or as 'hill' plants in the open, planting out after frosts at 24 in (60 cm) intervals in rows set 30 in (75 cm) apart. Harvest when large enough. Best fresh but can be stored for a few days. Recommended varieties: 'Athene' (greenhouse), 'Bush Champion' (hill).

eggplant
Tender annual. Grown from seed sown in spring and kept in a greenhouse or planted outside in a warm position at 24 in (60 cm) intervals in rows 24 in (60 cm) apart, once the frosts have passed. Good container plant. Harvest fruit when ripe. Best eaten fresh but can be kept for a few days in a refrigerator. Recommended varieties: 'Galine', 'Rima'.

endive (escarole)
Hardy annual. Sow in late spring or summer *in situ* in rows set 14 in (35 cm) apart. Grows best in cooler condions—its bitterness increases at higher temperatures. Thin seedlings to 10 in (25 cm). Cover the center of the plants with a plate or tile to blanch them. Harvest as required. Recommended varieties: 'Pancaliere', Full Heart Italian'.

fava bean
Hardy annual. Generally sown directly in the soil where it is to grow. Sow at 9 in (23 cm) intervals in rows set 12–36 in (30–90 cm) apart, depending on height of variety. Support taller varieties using cane pyramids or rows of canes. Harvest when the pods have swollen. Best eaten fresh but can be frozen. Recommended varieties: 'Aquadulce', 'Imperial Green Longpod', 'Meteor', 'The Sutton'.

fennel
Hardy perennial. Sow *in situ* or under glass from early summer onward. Thin to or plant at 12 in (30 cm) intervals in rows set 24 in (60 cm) apart. As bulbs swell, earth up around to blanch the leaves. Harvest when big enough for the table. Best eaten fresh, but can be frozen. Recommended varieties: 'Cantino', 'Sweet Florence'.

garlic
Hardy annual. Plant the bulbs in late autumn or spring at 6 in (15 cm) intervals in rows set 10 in (25 cm) apart. Harvest and dry in mid-summer. Dry after lifting and store in a cool frost-free place. Recommended varieties: often sold simply as garlic.

Jerusalem artichoke
Hardy annual. Plant the tubers 6 in (15 cm) deep at 12 in (30 cm) intervals in rows 4 ft (1.2 m) apart. Harvest from autumn onward. Leave in ground until required or lift and store in a cool, dark place. Recommended variety: 'Fuseau'.

kale
Hardy annual. Sow in seed bed or in trays in spring. Plant out in rows set 24 in (60 cm) apart at 18 in (45 cm) intervals. Harvest from late autumn onward. Eat fresh. Recommended varieties: 'Bornick', 'Fribor'.

kohlrabi
Hardy annual. Sow directly where it is to grow from spring onwards in rows set 12 in (30 cm) apart. Thin seedlings to 8 in (20 cm) intervals. Harvest when large enough. Eat as required, preferably while still quite small. Recommended varieties: 'Green Vienna', 'Purple Vienna', 'Rowel'.

leek
Hardy annual. Sow in spring in seed bed or in trays/modules. Grows well in cooler conditions, but will tolerate higher temperatures if kept well watered. Plant out in rows 12 in (30 cm) apart at 6 in (15 cm) intervals. Harvest when large enough. Leave in the ground until required. Recommended varieties: 'Autumn Mammoth-Goliath', 'Cortina'.

lettuce
Tender/hardy annual. Sow directly where it is to grow, or in trays under glass from spring onward. Thin to or plant out at 9 in (23 cm) intervals in rows set 12 in (30 cm) apart. Harvest when large enough. Lift whole plant as required. For cut-and-come-again varieties, harvest individual leaves as needed. Recommended varieties: 'Bubble', 'Little Gem', 'Lollo Rossa', 'Winter Density'.

onion
Hardy bulb. Can be grown from seed or sets (small bulbs). Plant sets in spring at 4 in (10 cm) intervals in rows set 12 in (30 cm) apart. Sow seed in winter under glass and plant out seedlings at intervals as above. Harvest in summer when the leaves begin to yellow. Dry in the sun and then store in a cool, frost-free place. Recommended varieties: 'Giant Fen Globe', 'Sturon'.

parsnip
Hardy annual. Sow where it is to grow in early spring in rows set 12 in (30 cm) apart. Thin seedlings to 6–8 in (15–20 cm) apart. Harvest from late autumn onward. Mark their position and leave in the ground until required—their flavor is improved by frost. Recommended varieties: 'Javelin', 'Tender and True'.

pea
Tender annual. Sow in double rows from spring onward at 2 in (5 cm) intervals. Rows should be 2–3 ft (60–80 cm) apart depending on variety. Support taller varieties with sticks or netting. Harvest once pods swell. Best eaten fresh but can be frozen. Recommended varieties: 'Early Onward', Hurst Greenshaft', 'Oregon Sugar Pod'.

pepper
Tender annual. Sow in spring under glass and continue to grow under glass except in warm or sheltered areas. Plant 18–24 in (45–60 cm) apart in the open, closer in pots or growing bags. Harvest green or when ripe. Best eaten fresh but can kept for a week or so in cool conditions. Recommended varieties: 'Ace', 'Carnival', 'Gold Star'.

potato
Tender annual. Plant seed tubers 12–15 in (30–38 cm) apart in a trench 6 in (15 cm) deep from early spring onward. Adjacent rows should be 30 in (75 cm) apart . Draw up the soil around the growing stems and protect from frost. Harvest from summer onward. Recommended varieties: 'Foremost' (early), 'Estima' (second early), 'Cara' (maincrop), 'Pink Fir Apple' (salad).

pumpkin
Tender annual. Sow seed under glass in spring and plant out after frosts have passed at 3–6 ft (90 cm—1.8 m) intervals depending on variety. Harvest when large enough and before frosts. Some varieties can be hardened off in the sun and then stored in a cool place for several months. Recommended varieties: 'Atlantic Giant' (for size), 'Crown Prince' (for flavor).

radish
Tender/hardy annual. Sow *in situ* from spring onward in rows set 6 in (15 cm) apart. Thin seedlings to 1–2 in (2.5–5 cm) apart. Harvest when large enough. Eat fresh, pulling as required. Recommended varieties: 'French Breakfast', 'Prinz Rotin', 'Sparkler'.

rhubarb
Hardy perennial. Plant crowns in winter at 30–36 in (75–90 cm) intervals. Early crops can be raised each year by forcing—covering the plants with a special pot or a bucket. Harvest the stalks from spring onward. Best fresh, but can be frozen or canned. Recommended varieties: 'Champagne', 'Timperly Early'.

rutabaga
Hardy annual. Sow *in situ* in early summer in rows set 18 in (45 cm) apart. Thin seedlings to 12 in (30 cm) intervals. Harvest from late autumn onward. Can be left in ground until required or stored in trays of just-moist sand in frost-free position. Recommended varieties: 'Best of All', 'Marian'.

salsify
Hardy annual. Sow where it is to grow in spring in rows set 25 cm (10 in) apart. Thin the seedlings to 15 cm (6 in) intervals. Harvest from late autumn onwards. Can be left in ground until required or stored in trays of just-moist sand in frost-free position.

scallion
Hardy annual. Sow *in situ* in rows set 6–8 in (15–20 cm) apart. Thin if necessary to 1 in (2.5 cm) apart. Harvest when big enough. Pull and eat as required. Recommended varieties: 'White Lisbon', 'Winter Over'.

scarlet runner (climbing bean)
Tender annual. Sow *in situ* or in individual pots under glass from late spring onward. Plant out after frosts. Thin or plant at 10–12 in (25–30 cm) intervals with rows set 3–4 ft (90–120 cm) apart. Support the beans on poles or netting. Harvest from mid-summer onward. Best used fresh but can be frozen. Recommended varieties: 'Enorma', 'Liberty'.

sea kale
Hardy perennial. Plant crowns in spring 2 in (5 cm) deep at 15 in (38 cm) intervals in rows set 18 in (45 cm) apart. Cover the plant in mid-winter with a light-proof pot and harvest the blanched stalks in early spring. Eat as it matures. Recommended varieties: usually sold simply as sea kale.

shallot
Hardy bulb. Plant the bulbs just below the surface at 6 in (15 cm) intervals with 12 in (30 cm) between rows. Harvest in summer. Dry off in the sun and then store in a cool, frost-free place. Recommended varieties: 'Dutch Yellow', 'Hative de Niort', 'Sante'.

spinach
Tender/hardy perennial. Sow where it is to grow in spring onward in rows set 12 in (30 cm) apart. Thin the seedlings to 6 in (15 cm). Harvest when leaves large enough. Best used fresh but can be frozen. Recommended varieties: 'Monnopa', 'Sigmaleaf'.

Swiss chard
Hardy annual. Sow in spring where it is to grow in rows set 18 in (45 cm) apart. Thin seedlings to 12 in (30 cm) intervals. Harvest when leaves are large enough. Cut leaves as required; cover with cloches in colder areas. Recommended varieties: 'Foordhook Giant', 'Lucullus', 'Rhubarb Chard'.

tomato
Tender annual. Grow from seed under glass in spring and either continue under glass in pots or grow bags, or plant out after frosts have passed. Plant at 24 in (60 cm) intervals. Cordon varieties need support and should have any side shoots removed. Bush varieties need neither. Pick when ripe. Can be frozen, canned, or dried. Recommended varieties: 'Dombito', 'Gardener's Delight' (cherry), 'Tigerella', 'Ida Gold' (bush), 'Totem' (bush).

turnip
Hardy annual. Sow in spring where they are to grow in rows set 12 in (30 cm) apart. Thin to 6 in (15 cm) intervals. Harvest when large enough. Can be left in ground until required or stored in trays of just-moist sand in a frost-free position. Recommended varieties: 'Golden Ball', 'Purple Top Milan', Snowball'.

zucchini
Tender annual. Sow in individual pots under glass. Plant out after frosts at 24 in (60 cm) intervals in rows 36 in (90 cm) apart. Harvest when small. Best eaten fresh but can be frozen. Recommended varieties: 'Astoria', 'Early Gem', 'Supremo'.

FRUIT

Most fruit needs a sunny position that is open yet protected from strong winds. The soil should be well prepared because the plants are likely to stay in the same place for many years. Remove all weeds and add plenty of well-rotted organic material, such as compost or farmyard manure. Plant any time between mid-autumn and early spring, as long as the weather is neither too wet nor too cold.

Fruit trees may be sold as maiden whips or maiden feathers. "Maiden" refers to grafted trees that are in their first year; "whips" are trees that have yet to grow any side shoots. A "feathered" tree is one that has side shoots.

In order to control the size and shape of a fruit tree, one type of tree may be grafted onto the rootstock of another. Some trees are also far easier to grow when grafted than from cuttings. Only closely-related plants can be grafted. The graft is accomplished by a union of the rootstock (the roots and a length of stem) from one plant, and the scion (a length of stem) from the plant to be raised. The whip and tongue technique is commonly used with fruit trees. Make mirror-image cuts in the rootstock and scion. Push them together firmly and bind the join with grafting tape. Remove the tape when the visible surfaces begin to callous (grow over).

Keep the soil at the base of trees and bushes weed-free, but avoid hoeing too deep and disturbing the roots. Top-dress the soil in autumn and spring with well-rotted organic material. Protect ripening fruit from bird attack by enclosing the plants in a fruit cage or loose netting. In some areas it will also be necessary to protect emerging buds from birds, but it is usually better to allow birds access outside the fruiting season because they will remove insect pests. If insects are a continuous problem, they should be dealt with using either organic or chemical means: seek advice from your local nursery.

Most fruit needs to be harvested once it has fully ripened, although fruit for storing is often best picked slightly before it ripens. Apples, pears, and quinces are the only fruit generally stored in the natural state. Other fruit may be frozen or canned.

apple
Can be grown as trees, bushes, cordons, dwarf pyramids, espaliers, fans, or poles. Harvest in autumn. Many varieties can be stored in cool, frost-free conditions.

apricot
Can be grown as bush trees or fans, preferably against a wall. Harvest in early autumn. Best eaten fresh, but can be dried or canned.

blackberry
Grown on canes supported on wires. Harvest from early summer onward. Best used fresh but can be frozen or canned.

black currant
Grown as bushes in cooler regions only. Harvest in summer. Best used fresh but can be frozen or canned.

blueberry
Grown as bushes. Harvest in summer onward. Best used fresh but can be frozen or canned.

cherry
Can be grown as trees, bush trees, or fans. Harvest in mid-summer. Best used fresh but can be frozen or canned.

damson plum
Can be grown as trees, bush trees, and fans. Harvest autumn onward. Best used fresh but can be frozen or canned.

fig
Can be grown as trees, bush trees, or fan, preferably against a wall. Harvest in autumn. Best eaten fresh but can be dried.

gooseberry
Grown as bushes, cordons, or standards. Harvest in summer. Best used fresh but can be frozen or canned.

grape
Grown as a vine on supports or against a wall. Harvest in autumn. Best eaten fresh, but can be turned into wine.

loganberry
Grown as canes against wire supports. Harvest in late summer. Best used fresh but can be frozen or canned.

nectarine
Grown as bush trees or fans, preferably against walls. Harvest early autumn. Best eaten fresh.

peach
Grown as a bush-tree or fan, preferably against a wall. Harvest early summer. Best eaten fresh.

pear
Grown as trees, bushes, cordons, espaliers, fans, or poles. Harvest in autumn. Best eaten fresh but can be stored in a cool place.

plum
Grown as trees, bush trees, and fans. Harvest late summer onward. Best used fresh but can be frozen or canned.

quince
Grown as trees, preferably in moist soil. Harvest late autumn. Can be stored.

raspberry
Grown as canes against wire supports.
Harvest from early summer onward. They
are best used when very fresh but can be
frozen or bottled.

red currant
Grown as bushes, cordons, fans, or
standards. Harvest in summer. Best used
fresh but can be frozen or canned.

strawberry
Grown as hardy perennials in the ground or
in containers. Harvest from early summer
onward. Best used fresh but can be frozen
or canned.

white currant
Grown as bushes, cordons, fans, or
standards. Harvest in summer. Best used
fresh but can be frozen or canned.

CULINARY HERBS

Herbs can be grown in a dedicated herb
garden, in the vegetable plot, mixed in with
ornamental plants in decorative borders, or
in pots. They generally like a free-draining
soil that is not too rich. Thoroughly prepare
the ground in autumn ready for spring
planting. Remove all weeds and add organic
material to improve the soil's structure but
do not add any extra fertilizer; there will be
enough feed in the humus.

Plant in spring, watering thoroughly.
Allow plenty of space for shrubby plants,
such as the sages, to spread. Some herbs,
including mint, are notorious spreaders and
must be contained in some way to prevent
their invading other plants.

Best quality herbs are obtained by
picking the leaves when still young,
preferably before the plants flower. After
this, the leaves may still be usable on some
plants, such as thyme, but on others they
become tired and tough. Once herbaceous
plants have flowered, they tend to look
bedraggled and should be cut back. Annuals
can be removed. However, if you want the
seeds, leave a few old flowering stems until
the seed has ripened. Do not eat or cook
with seed that has been sold for sowing
because this may have been treated with a
coating of chemical fungicide or pesticide.

Hang bunches of stems to dry in a warm,
airy place out of direct sunlight. Drying in an
oven is too quick. Hang bunches of seed
heads in muslin bags in a warm, airy place.
When leaves and seed are dry, store them in
air-tight, light-proof containers. Herbs can
be frozen in plastic freezer bags, and small
quantities can be frozen in ice cubes for later
use; first chop the leaves and then add them
to water in an ice cube tray. The whole ice
cube can later be added to a dish.

In the list below, only the most common
reason, or reasons, for growing a herb are
given: many can also be grown for other
parts of the plant that have decorative,
medicinal, or other value.

Allium schoenoprasum (chives)
Perennial bulb. 12 in (30 cm) high. Grown
for its leaves. Buy a container plant or divide
an existing one in spring. Plant out 8 in (20
cm) apart. Harvest as required. The leaves
can be dried or frozen for storage.

Anethum graveolens (dill)
Annual. Up to 5 ft (1.5 m) high. Grown for
its leaves and seed. Sow *in situ* from spring
onward. Thin to 10 in (25 cm) intervals.
Harvest leaves when young and seed when
ripe. Dry leaves and seeds for storage.

Anthriscus cerefolium (chervil)
Annual. 15 in (38 cm) high. Grown for its
leaves. Sow *in situ* from spring onward for a
continuous supply. Thin to 8 in (20 cm).
Harvest leaves before flowering.

Armoracia rusticana (horseradish)
Hardy perennial. 2 ft (60 cm) high. Grown
for its roots. Plant a container plant or divide
an existing plant in spring. Plant at 18 in (45
cm) intervals. Harvest roots as required.
Leave in the ground until needed: in very
cold areas, lift a few roots and store in just-
moist sand in a frost-free place over winter.

Artemisia dracunculus (tarragon)
Tender/hardy perennial. 24 in (60 cm) high.
Grown for its leaves. Buy container plants or
take cuttings from an existing plant in
summer. Plant at 18 in (45 cm) intervals.
Harvest leaves as required. The leaves can be
dried or frozen for storage.

Borago officinalis (borage)
Annual. 30 in (75 cm) high. Grown for its
flowers and young leaves. Sow seeds in a pot
or *in situ.* Thin to or plant out at 12 in (30
cm) intervals. Harvest leaves young and
flowers when required. Flowers can be
frozen in ice cubes or crystallized.

Brassica spp. (mustard)
Annual. Up to 6 ft (1.8 m) high. Grown for
its seed and young leaves. Sow in spring,
thinning to 6 in (15 cm). Harvest salad leaves
a few days after sowing and seeds as they
ripen in late summer. Dry seed for storage.

Carum carvi (caraway)
Annual or biennial. 2 ft (60 cm) high. Grown
for its seed and leaves. Sow seed *in situ* in
autumn. Thin seedlings in spring to 8 in
(20 cm) intervals. Harvest leaves when young
and seed in late summer when ripe. The
seeds can be dried for storage.

Chamaemelum nobile (chamomile)
Hardy perennial. 10 in (25 cm) high. Grown
for its leaves. Sow in spring in pots, or divide
an existing plant at the same time of year,
and plant out at 6 in (15 cm) intervals.
Harvest leaves at any time. The leaves can be
dried for storage.

Coriander sativum (coriander)
Biennial. 2 ft (60 cm) high. Grown for its
leaves and seeds. Sow in autumn or spring *in
situ* and thin to 8 in (20 cm) intervals.
Harvest leaves as required and seeds when
ripe. Dry seeds and freeze leaves for storage.

Foeniculum vulgare (fennel)
Hardy perennial. 7 ft (2.2 m) high. Grown for
its leaves and seed. Sow in spring in pots or *in
situ*. Thin to or plant at 24 in (60 cm) intervals.
Harvest leaves as required, seed when ripe.
Dry seeds and freeze leaves for storage.

Hyssopus officinalis (hyssop)
Hardy shrub. 2 ft (60 cm) high. Grown for its
leaves. Buy as a container plant or take
cuttings from an existing plant in summer.
Plant at 2 ft (60 cm) intervals. Harvest leaves
as required; they can be dried for storage.

Laurus nobilis (bay)
Hardy evergreen shrub. Up to 15 ft (4.5 m)
high. Grown for its leaves. Buy as a container
plant or take cuttings in late summer and
plant out resulting plants when big enough.
Can be topiaried. Harvest leaves as required.
Dried leaves are sweeter than fresh ones.

Levisticum officinale (lovage)
Hardy perennial. 7 ft (2.2 m) high. Grown
for its leaves and seed. Buy a plant or sow
seed in autumn. Plant out at 30 in (75 cm)
intervals. Harvest leaves as needed and seed
when ripe. Dry or freeze leaves for storage.

Melissa officinalis (lemon balm)
Hardy perennial. 3 ft (90 cm) high. Grown
for its leaves. Buy a container plant or divide
an existing plant in spring. Plant out at 2 ft
(60 cm) intervals. Harvest leaves as required.
The leaves can be dried for storage.

Mentha spp. (mint)
Hardy perennial. 24 in (60 cm) high. Grown
for its leaves. Buy a container plant or divide
an existing plant. Plant at 30 cm (12 in)
intervals. Rampant spreaders, so best
contained in some way. Harvest leaves as
required and dry or freeze for storage.

Monarda didyma (bergamot)
Hardy perennial. 3 ft (90 cm) high. Grown
for its leaves. Buy as container plant or divide
an existing plant in spring. Plant at 2 ft (60
cm) intervals. Harvest leaves as required.
The leaves can be dried for storage.

Myrrhis odorata (sweet Cicely)
Hardy perennial. 30 in (75 cm) high. Grown
for its seeds and leaves. Sow in autumn or
spring either in pots or *in situ*. Plant out or
thin to 24 in (60 cm) intervals. Harvest leaves
while they are young and seed either while
they are still green or when they are fully
ripe. Dry unripe seed for storage.

Ocimum basilicum (basil)
Tender annual. 18 in (45 cm) high. Grown
for its leaves. Sow under glass or after frosts
in situ. Plant at or thin to 8 in (20 cm)
intervals. Harvest leaves as required. The
leaves can be dried for storage.

Origanum marjorana (marjoram)
Annual or tender perennial. 24 in (60 cm)
high. Grown for its leaves. Grow from seed in
spring. Plant out at 18 in (45 cm) intervals.
Harvest as required. The leaves can be dried
or frozen for storage.

Origanum vulgare (oregano)
Hardy perennial. 24 in (60 cm) high. Grown
for its leaves. Grow from seed or by division
of existing plant in spring. Plant out at
18 in (45 cm) intervals. Harvest as needed.
Leaves can be dried or frozen for storage.

Petroselinum crispum (parsley)
Biennial. 12 in (30 cm) high. Grown for its
leaves. Sow in spring *in situ* or in pots. Thin
to or plant out at 9 in (23 cm) intervals.
Harvest leaves as required and dry or freeze
for storage.

Pimpinella anisum (anise)
Annual. 12–18 in (30–45 cm) high. Grown
for seed and leaves. Sow *in situ* in spring.
Thin to 8 in (20 cm). Harvest as required.
Seeds can be dried and stored.

Rosmarinus officinalis (rosemary)
Hardy evergreen shrub. Up to 6 ft (1.8 m)
high. Grown for its leaves. Buy a container
plant or take cuttings in summer. Plant out
in spring at 5 ft (1.5 m) intervals. Harvest
leaves as required. The leaves can be dried
for storage.

Salvia officinalis (sage)
Hardy evergreen shrub. 30 in (75 cm) high.
Grown for its leaves. Buy a container plant or
take cuttings in summer. Plant out in
spring at 3 ft (1 m) intervals. Harvest the
leaves as required. The leaves can be dried
for storage.

Satureja hortensis (summer savory)
Annual. 18 in (45 cm) high. Grown for its
leaves. Sow in spring in pots or *in situ*. Plant
out or thin to 9 in (23 cm) intervals. Harvest
leaves as required and dry for storage.

Satureja montana (winter savory)
Hardy shrub. 18 in (45 cm) high. Grown for
its leaves. Buy as a container plant or take
cuttings from an existing plant in summer.
Plant out at 18 in (45 cm) intervals. Harvest
leaves as required and dry for storage.

Thymus spp. (thyme)
Hardy shrub. Up to 12 in (30 cm) high.
Grown for its leaves. Buy as a container plant
or take cuttings from an existing plant in
summer. Plant out at 12 in (30 cm) intervals.
Harvest leaves as required. The leaves can be
dried for storage.

DECORATIVE AND OTHER
EDIBLE PLANTS

A kitchen garden commonly contains plants
other than just crops. Some are chosen for
their decorative value and are mixed in with
the food plants to add visual interest
throughout the year; others are grown
because they attract beneficial insects to the
garden; and still other species, which are not
considered to be food plants, have edible
flowers and are worth growing for use in
salads or just as a garnish. The following list
gives details of just a few such plants.

Allium schoenoprasum (chives)
Perennial bulb. 12 in (30 cm) high. Grown
in the herb garden for its leaves, but also has
attractive, edible purple flowers.

Allium tuberosum (Chinese chives)
Perennial bulb. Up to 18 in (45 cm) high.
Grown in the herb garden for its leaves, but
also has attractive, edible, white flowers. It
makes a perfect plant for edging beds.
Remove flower stalks after flowering.

Althea rosea (hollyhock)
Short-lived perennial/hardy annual. Up to
7 ft (2.2 m) high. Grown in old-fashioned
cottage gardens for its towering flower
spikes. The flowers are edible. Remove after
flowering if it is suffering from rust.

Amaranthus giganticus (leafy amaranth)
Tender annual. Up to 2 ft (60 cm) high.
Exotic plant with colorful tassels of flowers.
The leaves are edible. Sow *in situ* after the
frosts have finished or start under glass.

Amaranthus hypochondriacus (grain amaranth)
Tender annual. Up to 10 ft (3 m) high.
Towering plant with shaggy tassels of colorful
flowers. Grown for its decorative qualities
and edible seeds. Sow *in situ* after frosts have
passed or start under glass.

Atriplex hortensis (orache)
Hardy annual. Up to 6 ft (1.8 m) high. A tall,
decorative plant with red stems and foliage.
The young leaves can be eaten like spinach.
Will self-sow if left to seed.

Bellis perennis (English daisy)
Perennial/hardy biennial. Up to 6 in (15
cm) high. A low plant with white, pink, or
red edible flowers, ideal for edging beds.
Sow *in situ* or in trays and plant out in spring.

Borago officinalis (borage)
Annual. 30 in (75 cm) high. A herb grown
for its flowers and young leaves. It has a lax
habit and flops over other plants but it is
valuable in the decorative garden for its gray
foliage and blue flowers. Sow seeds in a pot
or where it is to grow. Will self-sow.

Buxus sempervirens (box)
Shrub. Very useful for low hedging. Plant at 8
in (20 cm) intervals; trim as they reach the
shape of the required hedge. Also good for
topiaried accent plants, either in the ground
or in containers.

Calendula officinalis (pot marigold)
Hardy annual. Up to 18 in (45 cm) high.
Grown in the herb garden for its leaves and
bright orange flowers. Sow *in situ* in autumn
or spring. If left it will self-sow.

Chenopodium bonus-henricus (Good King Henry)
Perennial. Up to 18 in (45 cm) high. A leafy
plant that looks like a weed but is grown for
its young leaves that are eaten like spinach in
spring. Grow from seed or by division.

Chenopodium giganteum (tree spinach)
Hardy annual. Up to 8 ft (2.5 m) high. Very
fast growing, tall plant with green leaves that
take on a reddish tinge. The leaves can be
eaten like spinach. Sow where it is to grow. It
is likely to self-sow prodigiously.

Curcubita (ornamental gourd)
Tender annual. Up to 6 ft (1.8 cm) high.
Ornamental varieties of squashes and
pumpkins cannot be eaten but make very
decorative climbing or trailing plants. Start
under glass and plant out after frosts.

Fragaria vesca (alpine strawberry)
Hardy perennial. Up to 25 cm (10 in) high.
Strawberry plants with delicious miniature
fruit that flower and fruit over a very long
period and make ideal plants for edging a
bed. Grown from divisions or seed.

Helianthus annuus (sunflower)
Hardy annual. Up to 10 ft (3 m) high. Tall
decorative plants grown for their flowers and
edible seed and petals. Sow *in situ* or in pots.

Hemerocallis (day lily)
Hardy perennial. Up to 4 ft (1.2 m) high.
Day lilies are attractive but take up quite a lot
of space. The flowers are colorful and good
to eat in salads or stir-fried while they are still
in bud. Plant out divisions in spring.

Humulus lupulus aureus (golden hop)
Hardy perennial. Up to 15 ft (4.5 m) high.
Rapid climbers perfect for covering posts or
trellises. The young shoots are a delicacy
when cooked like asparagus, and the female
flowers (hops) can be used for beer-making.
Plant out divisions in spring.

Laurus nobilis (sweet bay)
Hardy evergreen shrub. Up to15 ft (4.5 m)
high. Grown as a herb for its leaves. Highly
decorative when cut into a ball or other
topiary shape. Grow from seed or cuttings.

Lavandula angustifolia (lavender)
Hardy shrub. Up to 2 ft (60 cm) high. Grown
for its appearance and scent; the flowers can
be used to flavor and perfume food. Grow
from cuttings.

Malus sylvestris (crab apple)
Hardy tree. Up to 20 ft (6 m) high.
Decorative blossom in spring that is useful as
a pollinator for other apple trees. The small
fruit are useful for making preserves.

Papaver somnniferum (opium poppy)
Hardy annual. Up to 4 ft (1.2 m) high. A
decorative plant of no culinary value. A
slender plant with pink, purple, red, or white
flowers that self-sow.

Rosa (rose)
Climber or shrub. Up to 20 ft (6 m) high.
Decorative plants useful for growing over
arches and up through old trees. The hips of
wild varieties can be used for syrup and the
flowers are edible.

Tagetes erecta (marigold)
Tender annual. Up to 12 in (30 cm) high.
A colorful (gold and mahogany) addition
to the vegetable garden, but also grown to
deter whitefly and other pests. Grow from
seed under glass; plant out after frosts
have passed.

Tropaeolum majus (nasturtium)
Tender annual. Up to 2 ft (60 cm) high. A
colorful climber and trailer that can be used
to cover bare ground. Its flowers can be used
in salads. Grow seed under glass and plant
out after frosts have passed.

Viola odorata (sweet violet)
Hardy perennial. Up to 6 in (15 cm) high.
Grown for its violet, purple, or white flowers
that can be used as a table decoration or the
petals added to sweets. It can be crystallized.
Plant out from divisions or seed.

Viola tricolour (Johnny-jump-up)
Hardy perennial. Up to 6 in (15 cm) high.
Miniature pansies that have a habit of self-
sowing around the vegetable garden. The
petals are edible. Grow from seed.

Viola x *wittrockiana* (pansy)
Hardy perennial. Up to 6 in (15 cm) high.
Valuable as an edging or decorative plant.
The petals are edible. Can be grown from
seed or cuttings.

useful addresses

Plants, seeds and trees

Adams County Nursery, Inc.
P.O. Box 10826
Nursery Lane
Aspers, PA 17304
www.acnursery.com

Allen, Sterling & Lothrop
191 US Route 1
Falmouth, ME 04105
(207) 781-4142

Dacha Barinka
46232 Strathcona Road
Chilliwack, BC,
Canada V2P 3T2
(604) 792-0957

Bay Laurel Nursery
2500 El Camino Real
Atascadero, CA 93422
(805) 466-3406

Berton Seeds Company, Ltd.
4260 Weston Road
Weston, ON,
Canada M9L 1W9
(416) 745-5655

W. Atlee Burpee & Company
300 Park Avenue
Warminster, PA 18974-0001
(800) 888-1447
www.burpee.com

The Cook's Garden
P.O. Box 515
Londonderry, VT 05148-0515
(800) 457-9703
www. cooksgarden.com

Dabney Herbs
P.O. Box 22061
Louisville, KY 40252
(502) 893-5198
www.dabneyherbs.com

**Eden Organic Nursery
Services, Inc.**
P.O. Box 4604
Hallandale, FL 33008
(954) 455-0229
www.eonseed.com

Four Winds Growers
P.O. Box 3538
Fremont, CA 94539
www.fourwindsgrowers.com

Garden City Seeds
778 Highway 93 North
Hamilton, MT 59840
(406) 961-4837

The Gourmet Gardener
8650 College Boulevard
Overland Park, KS 66210
(913) 345-0490
www.gourmetgardener.com

Island Seed Company
P.O. Box 4278, Depot 3
Victoria, BC,
Canada V8X 3X8

Johnny's Selected Seeds
Route 1, Box 2580,
Foss Hill Road
Albion, ME 04910-9731
(207) 437-9294
www.johnnyseeds.com

Henry Leuthardt Nurseries, Inc.,
P.O. Box 666
Montauk Highway
East Moriches, NY 11940
(516) 878-1387

Mellinger's
2310 W. South Range Road
North Lima, OH 44452

Mountain Valley Growers
38325 Pepperweed Road, Squaw
Valley, CA 93675
(209) 338-2775
www.mountainvalleygrowers.com

Richters Herbs
357 Highway 47
Goodwood, ON,
Canada L0C 1A0
(905) 640-6677
www.richters.com

**Rocky Meadow Orchard
& Nursery**
360 Rocky Meadow Road N.W.
New Salisbury, IN 47161
(812) 347-2213

**Santa Barbara Heirloom
Nursery, Inc.**
P.O. Box 4235
Santa Barbara, CA 93140-4235
(805) 968-5444
www.heirloom.com

Seeds of Change
P.O. Box 15700
Santa Fe, NM 87506-5700
(888) 762-7333
www.seedsofchange.com

Shepherd's Garden Seeds
30 Irene Street
Torrington, CT 06790
(860) 496-9624, 482-3638
www.shepherdseeds.com

**Southern Exposure Seed
Exchange**
P.O. Box 170
Earlysville, VA 22936
www.southernexposure.com

Story House Herb Farm
587 Erwin Road
Murray, KY 42071
(502) 753-4158

Thompson & Morgan
P.O. Box 1308
Jackson, NJ 08527

West Coast Seeds, Inc.
8475 Ontario Street, Unit 206
Vancouver, BC,
Canada V5X 3E8
(604) 482-8800
www.westcoastseeds.com

Arbors, ornaments, and trellises

BowBends
P.O. Box 900
Bolton, MA 01740-0900
(508) 779-6464

Cincinnati Artistic Wrought Iron
2943 Eastern Avenue
Cincinnati, OH 45226

Garden Arches
P.O. Box 4057-B
Bellingham, WA 98227

The Garden Architecture Group
631 North Third Street
Philadelphia, PA 19123

Garden Concepts, Inc.
P.O. Box 241233
Memphis, TN 38124-1233
(901) 756-1649

Garden Trellises, Inc.
P.O. Box 105
LaFayette, NY 13084-0105
(315) 498-9003
www.GardenTrellises.com

**Heritage Garden Furnishings
and Curios**
1209 E. Island Highway 6
Parksville, BC
Canada V9P 1R5
(250) 248-9598

The Home Depot
for nearest store, contact:
(800) 430-3376 (US)
(800) 668-2266 (CAN)or
www.HomeDepot.com

Kinsman Company, Inc.
P.O. Box 357
Old Firehouse, River Road
Point Pleasant,
PA 18950-0357
(800) 733-4146
www.kinsmangarden.com

Smith & Hawken
P.O. Box 6907
Florence, KY 41022-6900
(800) 777-5858
www.Smith-Hawken.com

Stillbrook Horticultural Supplies
P.O. Box 600
Bantam, CT 06750-0600
(800) 414-4468
www.stillbrook.com

Sumerset Arbors
P.O. Box 7243
Beaumont, TX 77726-7243
(800) 645-3391

Sycamore Creek
P.O. Box 16F
Ancram, NY 12502

credits

The publishers would like to thank the following garden owners and designers for allowing their gardens to be photographed:

Chenies Manor, Buckinghamshire, Mrs Macleod-Matthews
Clinton Lodge, Sussex, Mr & Mrs Collum
Gopsall Pottery, Winchelsea, Sussex, Mike Crosby Jones
Hollington Nurseries, Berkshire, Simon & Judith Hopkinson
Old Place Farm, Kent, Mr & Mrs Jeffrey Eker
Rofford Manor, Oxfordshire, Mr & Mrs Mogford
Terence Conran's Chef Garden, RHS Flower Show, Chelsea
Warren Farm Cottages, Hampshire, Dr & Mrs Mitchell
West Dean Gardens, Sussex, Edward James Foundation
Whole Earth Foods, Portobello Rd, London

Jonathan Buckley would particularly like to thank Judith and Simon Hopkinson at Hollington Nurseries and Sarah Wain at West Dean for their help throughout this project.

index

acknowledgments

The author would like to thank all those involved in bringing this book to fruition: Anne Ryland whose idea it was and who commissioned me to write it; Marek Walisiewicz for his editing and suggestions; Paul Reid for his design that brings the whole thing to life; the illustrator, Richard Bonson, who has gone to great pains to turn rough sketches into images; and last, but not least, Jonathan Buckley, whose brilliant photographs make the book.

Thanks also go to all the owners who allowed Jonathan to photograph their wonderful vegetable gardens for this book.